Jenny Gibbs

Interior design

Laurence King Publishing

Introduction

6 Who this book is for
8 The role of an interior designer
9 Other professionals in the field
12 How to use this book

I Context

14 The value of historical study
14 The profession through time
26 The industry in the twenty-first century
26 Market segmentation and specialization
31 Globalization
35 The role of the media
38 The language of interior design

II Pre-design work

40 The client/designer relationship
44 The brief
46 The survey
56 Preliminary research
58 Formulating a concept
64 Towards a design solution

III Planning and design

66 The principles of design
74 Practical planning
76 Integrating the services
86 Drawing up designs
92 Design illustration

IV Harmonizing the elements

96 Colour
104 Developing a decorative scheme
106 Suppliers and trade accounts
106 Texture
107 Pattern
108 Materials and finishes
116 Selecting furniture
118 Details and accessories
118 Sample boards
122 Preparing for the presentation

V Project coordination and management

124 Stages of a project
124 Stage one
126 Stage two
130 Stage three
134 Stage four

VI Design education and beyond

144 Have you got what it takes
145 Selecting a course of study
147 Entry requirements
148 The college syllabus
152 The graduate show
152 Assessment
154 The future of design education
155 The importance of qualifications
157 Finding employment

VII Careers

166 Residential design
166 Commercial design
175 The future of the industry

181 Glossary
184 Further reading
185 Useful addresses
186 Index
191 Credits and acknowledgements

LAURENCE KING

Published in 2005 by
Laurence King Publishing Ltd

71 Great Russell Street
London WC1B 3BP
United Kingdom
Tel: +44 20 7430 8850
Fax: +44 20 7430 8880
e-mail: enquiries@laurenceking.co.uk
www.laurenceking.co.uk

A catalogue record for this book is available from the
British Library.

ISBN-13   978-1-85669-428-5
ISBN-10   1-85669-428-3

Designed by Simon Osborne
Picture research by Claire Gouldstone
Printed in China

Front cover: Guest room corridor at the Palau Sa Font
Hotel in Palma Mallorca. Interior design by Hans-Jürgen
Pahl. Photo: Eberhard Hahne

Back cover: Seating area overlooking the lobby at the Side
Hotel in Hamburg. Interior design by Matteo Thun.
Photo: Klaus Frahm/Artur

Frontispiece: Mirabelle restaurant, London, refurbished by
architect and designer David Collins.

Introduction

This introduction explains the purpose of the book and how to use it. It also clarifies the role of the interior designer and introduces the other professionals with whom a designer is likely to collaborate during the course of a project.

Who this book is for

Since the walls of caves were first decorated with primitive paintings, it has been a natural instinct for humans to embellish their environment. For many people, the design, decoration and refurbishment of a home provide a wonderful outlet for creativity. In recent years, the media has played a key part in educating and informing the general public about all aspects of interior design. This has stimulated a great deal of interest in the subject as a whole, and has resulted in more discerning shoppers and clients in the interior design marketplace. As the pace of life continues to accelerate, there has been more emphasis on the home as a retreat, and the look and ambience of the home environment have become more important to individuals. In some sections of society, the home is also viewed as a status symbol, the ultimate expression of wealth and style. It is not surprising, therefore, that people are increasingly employing the services of interior designers and that interior design has itself become a very popular career option.

Globally, interior design is considered to be a growth industry, although since it is at the luxury end of the service market it is inevitably prey to economic ups and downs. Traditionally, the building industry has been a good barometer of a country's economy and when that area of business is damaged by a downturn, the interiors industry is often affected in turn. This should not discourage anyone from entering the interior design profession, however, since there are excellent opportunities for career progression and specialization in the industry. Furthermore, the practical and creative skills acquired through a design education make graduates highly employable in a number of different fields.

Humans have always felt a need to embellish their environment. Here, paintings in black pigment decorate the walls of the famous Chauvet caves in the Ardèche Valley, France (c. 25,000–17,000 B.C.).

While this book is aimed primarily at aspiring professional interior designers — including school leavers, design students and career changers — it should also appeal to the amateur enthusiast. In addition, it offers a practical source of reference for both practitioners in the industry who are looking to broaden their practice and pursue new opportunities and for those who teach or advise people who are entering or considering entering the interior design industry. Throughout, it highlights the opinions and comments of established professionals in the field.

Most books that are available on the subject tend to be of the glossy, 'coffee-table' variety that focus on particular styles or types of interior, with little explanation of the workings of the industry itself, the training required, or how a designer comes up with a creative response to a client's brief. This book covers the entire design process from start to finish within the context of global developments in the industry itself. In addition, it presents a balanced view of interior design education and discusses the qualities and skills needed

Interior design has become a truly global language. The low, clean lines and spontaneity of Scandinavian design, for example, have informed international interiors throughout the twentieth and early twenty-first centuries. Shown here is Ränangen House in Djursholm, Sweden, designed in the 1950s and still much admired today.

by students who wish to enter the industry. The book also works as a general guide to the range of job opportunities available. It is not a training manual as such, but offers an insight into how professional designers are trained and how successful designers reach their goals.

The role of an interior designer

The role of an interior designer is defined by the International Interior Design Association as follows:

> *The Professional Interior Designer is qualified by education, experience, and examination to enhance the function and quality of interior spaces. For the purpose of improving the quality of life, increasing productivity, and protecting the health, safety, and welfare of the public, the Professional Interior Designer:*
> + *analyzes the client's needs, goals and life and safety requirements;*
> + *integrates findings with knowledge of interior design;*
> + *formulates preliminary design concepts that are appropriate, functional and aesthetic;*
> + *develops and presents final design recommendations through appropriate presentation media;*
> + *prepares working drawings and specifications for non-load-bearing interior construction, materials, finishes, space planning, furnishings, fixtures and equipment;*
> + *collaborates with professional services of other licensed practitioners in the technical areas of mechanical, electrical, and load-bearing design as required for regulatory approval;*
> + *prepares and administers bids and contract documents as the client's agent;*
> + *reviews and evaluates design solutions during implementation and upon completion.*

The role of the interior designer is multifaceted. To cope with this, a designer needs to be efficient and disciplined, with good business skills, as well as flexible, creative and artistic. Interior design is a people-oriented industry, involving collaboration not only with clients but with other professionals, specialists and suppliers, and it is vital that the designer is a good communicator.

There are some essential attributes for any successful designer. Of course the sine qua non *is a high level of accomplishment in the mechanics of the trade: the space planning, the marshalling of materials, the understanding of colour. But this counts for nothing if it is not harnessed to a rigorous grasp of detail and a tenacious ability to get things done. Great schemes are soon forgotten if they are not implemented on time and in budget.*
Martin Waller (British) – director of Andrew Martin Designs and organizer of the annual international Designer of the Year Award

Other professionals in the field

In this technological and litigious age, an interior designer is unlikely to work on any project in isolation. A project requiring structural changes could involve a surveyor to establish the state of the building and, possibly, to conduct negotiations with adjoining owners affected by the building works. In some instances, it is the surveyor who liaises on behalf of the designer with planning officials for necessary permissions. A district surveyor needs to be informed of any project taking place that involves structural work even if planning permission is not required. In the event of major rebuilding works, conversion or extension work it will be necessary to liaise with officials such as a planning officer or fire officer.

From taking the client's brief and developing designs to overseeing a project right through to the installation of furniture, artworks and accessories, the role of the interior designer is multifaceted.

At the outset of a project, the designer needs to formulate a creative response to the client's brief, and a concept board such as this one is often used to evoke the essence of a design.

An architect might be involved in cases where substantial interior structural changes are required or an existing property is being extended. If calculations are needed to demonstrate that all loads within a building structure are safely constructed and properly accounted for, then a structural engineer or a mechanical engineer, who would design mechanical and electrical installations, such as lifts, heating, ventilation, air conditioning, sound or computer systems, might be brought in on a project.

It often makes good sense for a designer to work with a specialist lighting consultant on the lighting schemes for a project. Specialists for other services such as heating, ventilation, air conditioning, and computer and sound systems might also be involved. Similarly, bathroom and kitchen design specialists might be employed.

Once the project is under way, the designer will be working with individuals from many trades, including builders, plumbers, heating engineers, electricians, joiners, plasterers, painter/decorators, decorative paint specialists, wallpaper hangers, flooring contractors, curtain makers, upholsterers, French polishers and many others.

A designer specializing in office design would be required to provide comfortable and ergonomically sound working environments.

How to use this book

Across seven chapters, the book examines the interior design industry in context, explores the wide range of information, concepts and processes that a designer is likely to encounter, reviews the various employment possibilities and provides advice on securing the all-important first job.

Chapter 1, 'Context', presents an overview of the historical development of interior design and the key stylistic changes through the centuries. It looks at how the industry operates today from a global perspective and outlines the different market segmentations and specializations that exist in the profession.

Chapter 2, 'Pre-design Work', looks at the preliminary stages of a design project: the client relationship, methodology and the collation of information. It discusses how research is used to generate innovative ideas, which can then be developed into creative solutions.

Chapter 3, 'Planning and Design', sets out the principles of good design and details how to go about integrating the complex services that the modern home or commercial interior requires. One of the major changes in interior design practice has been that designers are expected to have considerable technical knowledge in order to work with the relevant specialists to accommodate the latest technologies in a space. The chapter also looks at the different ways of communicating design ideas and solutions.

Chapter 4, 'Harmonizing the Elements', considers the various ways in which the designer sources materials, finishes, furniture and accessories and develops a decorative scheme. It explains both the theoretical and psychological aspects of colour and discusses how designers make up sample boards to show clients how a scheme might look. Finally, it discusses how to prepare for the client presentation.

Chapter 5, 'Project Coordination and Management', provides a complete overview of the key stages of a project from start to finish and the related processes, including the difference between coordinating small, residential projects and managing larger, commercial ones.

Chapter 6, 'Design Education and Beyond', reviews the qualities and attitudes a designer should have and the skills and knowledge they need to acquire through training. It discusses the types of education and training on offer and how courses are structured. It also includes advice on putting together an appropriate CV and portfolio and finding employment. Finally, there are tips on what to expect from a first job.

Chapter 7, 'Careers', looks at the different career paths within the design industry and the opportunities for specialization and personal development. In addition, it reflects on possible future developments in the industry.

At the end of the book there is a glossary of terms, suggestions for further reading, and address lists for suppliers, organizations and places of research.

Context I

This chapter outlines the development of interior design and the major stylistic changes through history, and looks at how the industry operates today. It includes a brief review of the different market segmentations and specializations that have emerged with reference to international design and global opportunities and influences, and considers the role of the media in the industry.

The value of historical study

There has been considerable debate within the world of design education in recent times about the value of historical study in relation to interior design. Nowadays, it is generally accepted that the development of the major architectural and interior styles provides an immensely worthwhile area of study for the design student. It goes without saying that an interior designer should be reasonably well-versed in this area, aware of leading figures who have played a part in these developments and able to recognize key styles, but gaining a real understanding of how styles have developed through time cannot be underestimated. Furthermore, it is the context in which these styles have changed and the geographical, historical and political influences which have helped to bring about these developments that make this study so fascinating and help to promote an understanding of international cultural links and global influences.

The profession through time

The profession of interior design is a relatively new one, since historically the differences between architects, craftsmen, upholsterers and interior decorators have tended to be blurred. If we look at the interplay among these different professions through the centuries, an interesting pattern emerges.

The seventeenth century

In seventeenth-century Italy, the classicism of the Renaissance began to evolve into the theatrical and ornate baroque style. From here, the style spread throughout Europe, particularly flourishing in southern Germany, Austria, Spain and Portugal. When baroque started to emerge in France and England, few architects had any input in the actual interiors of the buildings they designed and major projects were more usually undertaken by specialist craftsmen who worked from the engravings of Italian architects.

Patrons played an important part in the development of interior design and architecture in the seventeenth century. This was particularly evident in France, where Henry IV placed craftsmen under royal protection, Louis XIII fostered a national style, and Louis XIV commissioned wonderful work at the palace of Versailles from architects such as François Mansart, Louis Le Vau and Charles Le Brun. Le Brun took Le Vau's rooms at Versailles and transformed them into something of real brilliance and it could be argued

Seventeenth-century style

The interior of the Charlottenburg Palace in Munich was designed by Dutch architect Arnold Nering in 1695–99 and is a wonderful example of the richness and drama of the baroque style. Baroque was particularly suited to public buildings such as churches and palaces.

Le Brun's stunning Hall of Mirrors at the Palace of Versailles, near Paris, became one of the most celebrated examples of palace architecture in seventeenth-century Europe.

Floors and ceilings were treated as integral parts of Inigo Jones' design of the Queen's House at Greenwich, England.

The huge canopy in St. Peter's, Rome, designed by Gianlorenzo Bernini in 1624–33, lends a strong baroque character to the space.

that he was the first full-service interior decorator. The elegance and comfort of French interiors, primarily intended for the aristocracy, were universally admired and influenced other European countries such as Sweden. In Holland, a more modest version of French style developed that was acceptable to the emergent middle-classes, and Dutch imported goods were very much in demand.

When the Stuarts were restored to the throne of England towards the end of the seventeenth century, Charles II and his courtiers favoured the continental baroque style, and the later rule of William and Mary of Orange resulted in further continental influence on English styles. Princesses of the House of Orange spread their enthusiasm for decorative details such as mirrors, massed porcelain and lacquerwork through their royal marriages.

William and Mary commissioned the highly talented Daniel Marot, who as a result of religious persecution had fled the French court, where he had been working, to design the interiors of parts of Hampton Court Palace. There, Marot successfully combined the skills of designer and decorator, as Le Brun had done, and his cohesive interiors can still be seen today. Huguenot refugees played an important part in English interior design development since many of them were highly skilled craftsmen. Inigo Jones, who was widely regarded as the founder of English classical architecture, also treated the interiors of his buildings as part of the whole.

The Thirty Years' War took a considerable toll on Spain and Germany and little architectural development took place in these countries during that time. Once both economies had recovered sufficiently for building to take place, tastes had changed considerably. Early versions of German baroque showed Italian influence, but gradually an indigenous rich and complex style emerged in south Germany and Austria. Highly ornate surface decoration was a feature of seventeenth-century Spanish architecture as in the façade of Santiago de Compostela or the Dos Aguas Palace at Valencia, but the more restrained Royal Palace in Madrid and the Royal Palace of La Granja by Filippo Juvarra were influenced by the more severe French baroque style.

The eighteenth century

In the early to mid-eighteenth century, the frivolous, exuberant rococo, which began in Paris where there was a new craving for informality away from the rigidity of court life, was particularly dependent for its interior styling on the skills of key craftsmen. One such was the Belgian master carver Jacques Verberckt, although Ange-Jacques Gabriel is the architect perhaps most closely associated with French rococo. The rococo style was embraced by the European aristocracy and foreign rulers and royalty consulted French architects on the construction and decoration of key buildings. Germany, in particular, took rococo to its heart, with architects such as Johann Balthasar Neumann designing highly ornamental palaces and churches. In Spain, architects incorporated elements of French rococo in their work but developed them to create distinctive regional styles.

The other major eighteenth-century style was the Palladian revival, which flourished in England. It was introduced by the architect Lord Burlington who brought back engravings by the sixteenth-century Venetian classical architect Andrea Palladio from a trip to Italy. The style was then adapted to suit English taste with the use of restrained baroque decoration within Palladian disciplines. This compromise was much influenced by William Kent whose designs for interiors such as Houghton Hall in Norfolk demonstrated that he was a superb interior designer as well as a skilled architect and furniture and landscape designer.

An illustration from Thomas Hope's inspirational book *Household Furniture and Decoration*, a major influence on interiors of the period.

A delightful plate from *Recueil de décorations intérieures* illustrates the distinctive design style that made Percier and Fontaine favourites of Emperor Napoleon.

One of the greatest exponents of the neoclassical style was Robert Adam, who treated interiors as an intrinsic part of the building design, even designing his carpets to match his intricate ceilings. Inspired by his studies in France and Italy, Adam was particularly skilled at developing original ideas from old styles. The neoclassical style was rational and coolly elegant, characterized by simple geometric forms, flat linear decoration and Greek and Roman ornament. It developed in Europe from the 1750s as a reaction to the extremes of rococo and spread from France to Spain, Holland, Germany and Scandinavia. In Italy and Spain, the baroque style was generally preferred, although in the late 1700s the Italian architect Piranesse produced some exemplary neoclassical designs. A notable neoclassical designer in Germany was Karl Friedrich Schinkel, who designed several influential buildings in Berlin, including the Old Museum, the National Theatre and the Royal Guards House. In America, neoclassical interiors were greatly influenced by the pattern books of architectural styles and, in particular, furniture from designers such as George

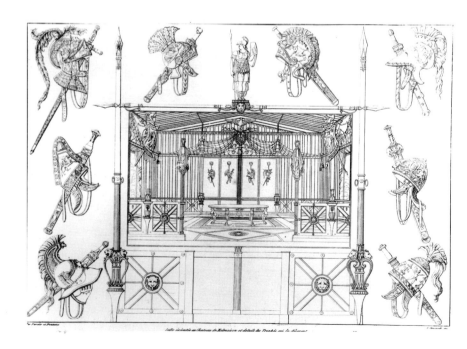

Eighteenth-century style

The use of hexagonal forms and the painted and gilded plasterwork in the central salon of the Stupinigi Palace (1729–33), outside Turin combines elements of both baroque and rococo style.

The curvaceous plasterwork and decorative cupids in the oval room at the Hôtel de Soubise in Paris are typical of French rococo style.

The white drawing room at Houghton Hall, England (1726–30), is a fine example of the beautifully proportioned work of William Kent. The room is decorated in harmony with the overall architectural design and includes a specially designed suite of furniture.

An interior of Le Malmaison, Paris, which was designed for Emperor Napoleon and his wife Josephine by architects Percier and Fontaine.

The sacristy of La Cartuja in Granada is a striking example of the highly ornate interiors that came into prominence in eighteenth-century Spain.

The magnificent staircase and surrounds in the Residenz in Würzburg, Germany, was designed by Neumann in 1735 and provides superb examples of the rich and highly decorative plasterwork and sculpture that typified the rococo style in Germany.

Hepplewhite and Thomas Chippendale. The new republic's third president, Thomas Jefferson, favoured simple classical forms which he used for the design of his own house, Monticello, in Virginia.

English cabinetmakers such as Thomas Sheraton and George Smith played an increasingly important role in the interior design and decoration of late eighteenth- and early nineteenth-century European and American interiors and often coordinated the interiors of major refurbishments and new buildings. One of the most successful furniture-making and interior decoration companies was Crace & Co, while publications such as Thomas Hope's book *Household Furniture and Decoration* (1807) and Rudolph Ackerman's *Repository of Arts* magazine made a huge impact on interior styles by making the public much more aware of decorative styles and possibilities.

Following the Nile campaign of 1798, Emperor Napoleon's prestige was at an all-time high in France. An admirer of the art of imperial Rome, Napoleon went to great lengths to encourage the arts in France, setting an example in patronage that was followed by the *nouveau riche*. He brought in the architects Charles Percier and Pierre-François-Léonard Fontaine to work on the royal palaces and they developed a highly original Empire style for these interiors which featured tent-style hangings and other references to the Napoleonic wars and the military campaigns. Through their book, *Recueil de décorations intérieures* (1812), their work became internationally influential.

The nineteenth century

As the nineteenth century progressed, a battle of styles led to increasingly excessive interiors and architecture throughout Europe and the US. While architects produced a bewildering range of building styles, upholsterer/decorators once again played an important part in the dressing of the interiors. Reaction against complex and cluttered interiors led to the return of simpler, lighter styles. It also saw the introduction of reform movements, such as the Arts and Crafts Movement in England, which placed great value on honest design, high-quality materials, craftsmanship and traditional skills, as well as beautiful surroundings. William Morris was a guiding light of the movement and designed his own textiles, wallpaper and furniture. These ideas were also influential in America, where they became known as the Craftsman style and were later championed by designers such as Elbert Hubbard and Gustav Stickley and the architect Frank Lloyd Wright.

In Europe, a distinctive and decoratively complex style appeared towards the end of the century which became known as art nouveau. With its asymmetric, curvilinear forms, it influenced architecture and interior design throughout Belgium, Austria, Germany, Italy and Spain. Key proponents of the style included Victor Horta in Belgium, Antoní Gaudí in Spain, August Endell in Germany and Charles Rennie Mackintosh in Scotland.

The eclectic Beaux Arts style that flourished in the US marked a new and important development in nineteenth-century interior design. Named after the many architects living in the US who had been trained at the Beaux

Nineteenth-century style

William Morris was one of the most influential figures of the Arts and Crafts Movement, advocating high-quality, handmade furniture and fabrics with natural dyes. This small bedroom in Kelmscott House, England, is typical of his style.

The repeated use of curving shapes and ornate decoration in the hall of Casa Calvert in Barcelona, Spain, exemplify Antoní Gaudí's highly individual style of architecture and design.

The ornate interiors of the Morse-Libby Mansion in Portland, ME, incorporated all the most modern technologies available, including gas lighting and central heating.

Twentieth-century style

In his home, Taliesen, in Wisconsin, Frank Lloyd Wright introduced drama with soaring spatial design and a bold use of raw materials.

Roquebrune in France was the home of influential art deco furniture and interior designer Eileen Gray.

Tugendhat House at Brno in the Czech Republic was designed by Mies van der Rohe, one of the leading lights of the Bauhaus school.

The American Bar in Vienna is a stunning example of an art deco bar interior, the ceiling design and use of motif being typical of the period.

Le Corbusier worked on Bauhaus principles and at the Villa Savoye in France installed roll-back glass walls to link the interior and exterior of the house.

The private dining room of the Colony Club in New York designed by Elsie de Wolfe, as illustrated in her book *The House in Good Taste*, 1913.

Left Since the late twentieth-century, restaurant design has become increasingly sophisticated. Terence Conran's restaurants have been at the forefront of this, and here at Plateau in Canary Wharf, London, the glazed ceiling maximizes the sense of space and light.

Arts School in Paris, the style encompassed a variety of historical styles, with comfort and harmony being the main priorities. Lavish interiors came equipped with mechanical communication devices, sophisticated bathrooms and kitchens, elevators and electrical systems. From this stage on, interior designers and architects had to be able to integrate the new technology into their projects.

The twentieth century

Art deco was a deliberately outrageous style that was fashionable in the inter-war period in the twentieth century. It took its name from the first decorative arts exhibition, *L'Exposition des Arts Décoratifs et Industriels Modernes*, held in Paris in 1925. Paris became a great centre for design in the early twentieth century courtesy of the work of the interior designers Jean-Michel Frank and Paul Poiret, and the interior and furniture designer Eileen Gray. In the late 1920s and 1930s, modernism displaced art deco, emerging from the Bauhaus, the influential German design school founded by Walter Gropius and later headed by architect Mies van der Rohe. The Bauhaus advocated functionalism with a minimum of colour, ornament and architectural features, and it required considerable design skills to pull off successfully.

Following the closure of the Bauhaus, disciples such as Serge Chermayeff and Eric Mendelsohn settled in Britain and the US where they influenced many architects and designers at that time. In France, the architect Le Corbusier adhered to Bauhaus principles and designed revolutionary houses that maximized light and space. As the twentieth century progressed, there emerged an increasingly pronounced gap between the architectural design of a building and its interior decoration. Dedicated interior decorators were really an innovation of the twentieth century and home decoration became an increasingly popular pastime. Many of these early interior decorators were members of the aristocracy who saw an opportunity to exploit their good taste and knowledge of the finer things by helping the new rich, who could afford lavish interiors but needed guidance in achieving the desired effects. In the US, Elsie de Wolfe led the way as one of the first female interior decorators of note.

World War II halted a boom period for architects and designers throughout Europe, a cessation that lasted a couple of decades. Afterwards, English interior decorators such as John Fowler and Nancy Lancaster brought their restrained and stylish skills to bear on many key country houses. What later became known as 'the country house look' burgeoned into an alarmingly full-blown and chintzy style in the latter half of the century and was particularly popular in the US. For a while there was a return to some of the classical disciplines and historical shapes and forms that had been elegantly introduced by designer David Hicks in the 1960s. One of the great champions of a more minimal and functional style, whose influence has extended into the twenty-first century on an international scale, is British designer and restaurateur Terence Conran.

Designer Ann Grafton's fresh, light interiors blend the best of New England and contemporary English country styles.

The industry in the twenty-first century

The practice of interior design has had to change radically over the last fifty years or so to adapt to today's requirements. Once the field of the talented, creative amateur, it is now a profession in its own right, requiring its practitioners to have technical knowledge combined with creative flair and the ability to deal with every aspect of a project. We are now seeing the rise of the interior designer/architect, well-qualified to maximize the use of space, introduce innovative materials and finishes, and discreetly incorporate the now essential technology.

To service this, there have been massive developments in design education, training, qualifications and associations. In some countries, there is still a way to go as the industry is polarized between being established, highly organized and viable in some areas (as it is in most of the US) and almost non-existent in other, more isolated or idiosyncratic areas. Although the industry in much of Europe is fast catching up with the US and is being taken more seriously, there is still a general perception that interior design is a frivolous occupation and that its practitioners are predominantly female or homosexual. In some quarters, interior designers are also held back by their own amateurish approach. Interior design is still predominantly an urban pursuit, and in major cities there is the erroneous assumption that the profession is just as highly valued outside of those cities.

In order to continue to raise standards of professionalism, it is important that designers become much more businesslike in their approach. There is also an argument for placing more emphasis on elements such as budgeting, business management and promotion within design education so that designers who eventually set up on their own have the know-how to grow from a small business into a medium-sized one.

Market segmentation and specialization

Traditionally, interior design has been divided into two main categories: residential and commercial. As the name implies, residential interior design focuses on the planning and specification of interior materials and products used in private homes. Residential interior designers must be aware of issues such as child safety, family traffic patterns, wiring and cable requirements, switching and security systems, as well as space requirements for home cinema electronics and computer hardware. There are also different challenges facing the design of multi-unit dwellings that also require consideration.

Commercial interior design focuses on the planning and design of public buildings and businesses, which can be anything from shops and restaurants to museums and hospitals. Historically, when a new profession emerges, specialisms develop in due course. Some designers concentrate on a specific area, such as entertainment (theatres, concert halls, theme parks and so forth), governmental or institutional, healthcare, hospitality (hotels, restaurants, bars, clubs and so on), offices, and retail (boutiques, department stores, shopping malls).

In addition to straightforward design projects for private clients, residential work may involve designing interior fittings for new housing developments or decorating show houses. Developers understand these days that quality design can mean the difference between profit and loss; where in the past the budget for the interior design element of a developed scheme would have been minimal, it is now regarded as a sound investment. Many developers are looking to sell lifestyles through interior design and are introducing luxury branding, be it heritage-based or contemporary chic. This can result in challenging and stimulating projects for designers. Some interior designers prefer to focus their expertise on particular types of property, such as country houses or period restoration.

Some European practices have built up good contacts overseas in areas such as the Middle East and concentrate their operations there, while other practices might take on work in a number of different countries. A practice might specialize in a particular area, such as kitchens, bathrooms or nurseries. It can make good commercial sense for a supplier of kitchen or bathroom fittings, for example, to also provide the design work for those spaces, and so a specialist design service can exist within a supply business.

Kitchen design is a booming specialist area in interior design and, due to increased public awareness, is becoming more and more creative and innovative in approach.

While interior designers often specify surface decoration in addition to designing the layout of a space, the whole area of materials, finishes, furniture and furnishings is so vast that an interior decorator who specializes in the cosmetic side of a design project might take on the decorative schemes, surface decoration, furniture and accessories. There are also specialist firms that provide these services. In some larger interior design practices, there is a fixtures, fittings and equipment (FF&E) department responsible for the purchase and supply of these elements, and there are an increasing number of specialist purchasing companies set up for the purpose.

There are many different types and sizes of design practices. In some instances an interior design practice may operate as part of a larger architectural practice. Many of the larger practices carry out commercial work only, while smaller and medium-sized set-ups may take on residential work but also the occasional boutique hotel, restaurant or suite of executive offices.

Opposite The imaginatively designed Nike Pavilion in London is intended to celebrate the company's technological expertise.

Having established a brand name, a well-known interior designer might decide to diversify into related areas such as product design or retail. Renowned designer Nina Campbell, for example, launched a successful range of products that included furniture, fabrics, glassware and, as illustrated here, wallpaper.

Designers' work is continually reflecting global influences and diverse styles are becoming increasingly fused as a result. This concept board, for example, features an image of the famous colossal heads at Easter Island in the Southeast Pacific.

In much of Europe, particularly the UK, it is unusual to find very large interior design practices. There are many successful operations with ten employees or even sole traders.

In the US, specialization is well-established, and with ever-increasing technological developments and very specific requirements of particular types of clients, this makes good sense, for example in areas such as medical services, hospitality, retail or exhibition work. In Europe, there are certainly practices that work only on hotels or hospitals, for example, but it is not unusual for commercial practices to take on a variety of projects.

Project management is increasingly becoming an area of specialization for all but the smallest projects and for this the designer would usually hand over to the project manager to implement the agreed designs.

In contrast to the increasing tendency to specialize, some design boundaries are becoming blurred as fashion designers, for example, have started to design product ranges for interiors such as glassware, china, cutlery, bedlinen and table linen. Likewise, many interior designers are beginning to encompass furniture, product or even fashion design in their work. A successful designer in any discipline, having established a good brand name has the perfect platform from which to develop an individual design range. Versace, Giorgio Armani, Ralph Lauren and John Rocha are all examples of fashion designers who have expanded into areas such as furniture design and homeware; Kelly Hoppen and Nina Campbell are interior designers who have moved into product design and retail. Interior designers are increasingly involved in promoting style, and in commercial projects they may be required to contribute to a company image through graphics or other types of branding.

Globalization

One of the great attractions of interior design is its flexibility. While styles and materials may vary in different parts of the world, the fundamental design skills always apply.

Members of professional interior design and architectural associations interact at international conferences, which provide the opportunity for designers worldwide to exchange views and ideas. New technology has revolutionized the design world and opened up easy communication for designers working on projects abroad so that they are no longer constrained by borders. It has also brought about improved administrative systems and the speedy transmission of trends. Many design set-ups have become virtual offices and are able to call upon the skills of others both nationally and internationally. The design world is continually growing and offering a variety of career opportunities for the trained interior designer.

The quality of light varies dramatically throughout the world, which is one of the reasons why it does not always work simply to reproduce a particular national style in a different country. The boarded ceiling, floor and walls in this house by Ralph Erskine in north Stockholm, however, is a look that could easily be adapted to other environments.

Above Designers seek inspiration from all over the world. In this shopping emporium in Hamburg, Germany, the style is inspired by the famous medina in Marrakesh.

Opposite A North African flavour has been introduced into this restaurant in Philadelphia (David Schefer Design) by applying deep spice colours to the plaster walls.

Style influences are themselves becoming global. In large cities, clients often like their homes to have an international look and there is a ready market for interior design and its products. Efficient and affordable travel has encouraged the appreciation of many different indigenous styles with the result that interior design has become a global enterprise, with influences seen from countries as wide-ranging as South Africa, Australia, Thailand and Indonesia. Some of the strongest influences worldwide have come out of Africa – colonial, Moroccan, Tunisian styles, as well as the look of half-timbered thatched game lodges and indigenous huts, all mixed up into a vibrant, ethnic, organic look that can be seen in fabrics, artefacts and accessories. Fuelling the market for this type of decoration and style has been a frustration with the homogenization of looks and materials and the desire for something crafted, tactile and textural with a heart and soul.

Yet while it is often argued that design has become a universal language, it is not always appropriate to import national design characteristics developed over eons to a place that has a different climate, quality of light and culture. While Scandinavian design, for example, is highly appropriate for local conditions, with all the available wood, the short days and silver light, it does not always work so successfully when applied elsewhere. Designers have to be wary that just because something is novel and thrilling it is not necessarily right, and they must remember that ethnicity is a quality to be respected.

The media has played a considerable part in the development of interior design, influencing styles and informing the general public. Here, a concept board is based around the style and personalities of the characters from the successful US television series *Sex in the City*.

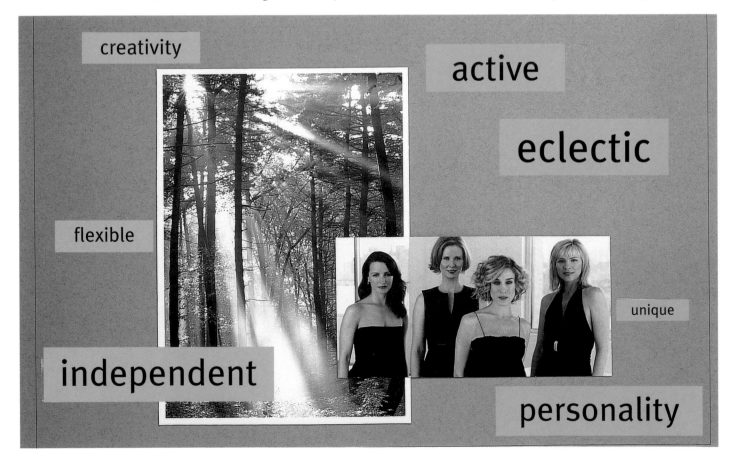

creativity

active

eclectic

flexible

unique

independent

personality

The role of the media

The media plays an immensely important part in the interior design industry, both in terms of helping to create a market for interior design and providing a valuable resource for the designer. There is some confusion about the media's role here, however. Does the media *create* trends or is its primary role one of observation and selection, bringing to public notice things that it believes to be true? For the print media, working as it does against voracious demands and schedules, there is often little time and resources for researched design journalism, with the result that magazines often follow one another rather than introduce new material and information.

There are signs that hospitality design, such as this striking cocktail lounge at the Gran Hotel Domine in Bilbao, Spain, is increasingly influencing residential interiors.

Design is a continuous learning process, and one should never stop educating the eye through art, travel, books, film and theatre.
Constanze von Unruh (German) – designer

The media also interacts with the design industry by producing potential clients through advertisements, feature articles, films and television programmes which create interiors that people want to acquire for themselves but need professional help to achieve.

The media, in all its forms, provides a diverse resource for the designer, who needs to be completely up to date not only with current trends but with the social, economic and political changes which may also influence the marketplace. A designer needs to be sensitive to the mood of the times and the way people are living, just as much as to specific popular styles.

As well as representing a mine of creative inspiration for designers, specialist books and magazines also contain useful information on sourcing for a trade reference library. The content of a trade reference library will depend to some extent on the type of work undertaken but could include catalogues of companies supplying items such as lighting, furniture, glass and mirror, kitchen and bathroom equipment, suspended ceilings, partitioning, wallcoverings, floor coverings and accessories. Many of these are listed as a supporting part of feature articles or as advertisements.

Clients or consumers may first be made aware of new trends at the top end of the market through exclusive interiors featured in magazines. Once a look catches on, it will then appear in an adapted form in more middle-market magazines, and related products will then become available on the high street. A direct result of the increased influence of the media has been that good design is much more appreciated and understood both in the commercial and residential sectors. The well-informed public is more sophisticated and demanding in its requirements and the high-street shops are responding by stocking higher-quality, more diverse design merchandise. Recently, the cutting-edge design of many new hotels and restaurants has led the way for new trends in the residential market and this, too, has been highlighted in the media.

The trendsetter is not someone who hides away in a darkened room and suddenly appears to announce a new design idea or style. A new trend is more likely to be a child of war, politics, conversation or the influence of other areas of the arts which a scholar or historian would be able to trace back to its roots.
Sue Crewe (British) – editor, *House & Garden* magazine

New influences are often the result of coincidence. One element may have taken a long time from conception to execution, such as a film or exhibition, and the other may have come about almost instantaneously, but the combination of the two results in a new trend. So while new concepts may come from media, travel, and the arts it is often the more oblique swing of the pendulum, the spirit of the times that causes styles to change and new trends to emerge. Good media should be able to identify the resonance behind a certain design by highlighting how it embodies a feeling of optimism or financial security, for example, or the influence of a new technology, book or exhibition.

This asymmetrical layout still retains a feeling of balance and allows users to circulate comfortably and naturally.

The language of interior design

One of the key functions of the designer is to interpret the ideas and identity of the client in order to provide an appropriate environment in which to live or work. The designer has the opportunity to convey all sorts of highly personal information about the client, including age, marital status, economic status, attitudes and possibly even physique, through the design of their surroundings. Some clients might wish the design to create a false impression in order to camouflage true personality traits or characteristics. So, although interior designers must be aware of current fashions and trends, it is important not to get lost in these, but rather to create a personal style for the client and to provide an interior that has an indefinable, attention-grabbing quality to set it apart from others.

Most interior schemes and plans are based on the basic principles of design, but some of the most innovative work may develop where a designer, while understanding and respecting those principles, intentionally pushes the boundaries by experimenting with different concepts and harmonies. This may include mixing linear and classical design, opening up spaces, creating unusual asymmetric layouts, specifying unusual materials or using common finishes or colours in an innovative way.

Interior design itself can also be used as a marketing tool. How a hotel or restaurant is designed and laid out, for example, is a crucial part of the way it promotes itself. Likewise, a shop window can be designed to draw customers into a shop, while the floor design and positioning of displays can manipulate them around the space in a way that increases the chances of their being confronted with potential purchases.

Pre-design work II

This chapter provides a realistic overview of the initial stages of a design project, including the client relationship, methodology and the collation of information. It describes how designers use research to spark innovative ideas and then develop these ideas to access their creativity and produce potential solutions. The emphasis in the pre-design stage is on flexibility.

The client/designer relationship

Interior design brings to mind a picture of designers sketching plans, playing with colour and texture to produce exciting schemes, or haunting specialist shops to track down unique pieces of furniture, decorative objects or detailing to customize their work. This can all certainly be a part of the job, but before the designer can consider any of the creative process, the pre-design work involves a great deal of information-gathering and methodology around which the project will be based. This process begins with the client relationship.

In the US, it is fairly normal practice to employ an interior designer to help design and decorate the home in the same way as any other professional might be employed to offer guidance in an area where the client does not have expertise. In many European countries, there is still some in-built resistance to the idea of using interior designers, perhaps because they are still viewed in some quarters as an expensive luxury that will increase costs considerably. In a country such as the UK, where individuality is prized, there is perhaps also the fear that the designer will impose too much of his or her own style or identity on a project. In the commercial world, however, the value of interior design has long been understood internationally.

It is clear that the ability of a designer to gain a thorough understanding of the client's requirements will be fundamental to the favourable outcome of a project, whether working with a corporate or private client. Many clients have very confused ideas about what they want and are not able to articulate their requirements fully. It is more usual for a client simply to list the problems they have and to put forward a random collection of ideas, rather than to present the designer with a thoroughly considered brief. It is therefore the designer's task to create and write the brief as the relationship develops. However, good design is not necessarily related to the actual quality of the client relationship. Some good designers are bad at articulating and conversing with a client, merely insisting that a client 'trusts' them, while for others it is important to make the whole process as enjoyable as possible for the client. The client relationship works on a number of different levels and there is never a right or wrong approach. In essence, it is a partnership to which both parties contribute, sparking off one other.

In recent years, there have been subtle changes in the relationship between designer and client, with the designer taking on more of a consultative, rather than prescriptive, role. The designer needs to understand the client's

Opposite Design considerations for a client may extend beyond family and guests to a much-loved pet. Here, there is easy access to a surrounding garden and carpets and rugs are kept to a minimum.

The choice of artwork and decoration in a home
can provide valuable clues to the client's taste,
lifestyle and even personality.

needs, personality and style and, in a commercial situation, to appreciate the wider economic context of these aspects. Mutual trust is a vital platform for smooth progression, and to achieve this, the designer needs to be able to speak the client's language and, above all, to listen to the client in order to interpret their ideas. This ability to observe and listen is of paramount importance when dealing with couples. The one who appears more dominant at meetings may not, for example, be the real decision-maker and the situation may be further complicated by the involvement of relatives, friends or domestic staff.

Good design is all about keeping a sense of balance and earning the client's respect. The designer needs to work in a cooperative way, adapting to the client's changing circumstances and priorities, responding rapidly to the client's concerns and keeping the client fully informed at every stage. In a commercial situation, although a designer may be liaising directly on a project with a director or committee, it is usually advantageous to take the time to consult fully with key staff to ensure that their requirements are considered wherever possible. Hotel housekeepers, for example, can prove a mine of helpful practical information for the designer as can restaurant staff and managers. When working in schools and colleges, designers can glean useful information not only from teaching and administrative staff but also from parents and pupils, and there is every chance that the board of governors will also need to approve everything. All of this requires a designer to adopt a flexible approach.

Collaboration with colleagues and other professionals engaged by the client or brought in to work on the project is a further aspect of the relationship. No one involved in a project will want to face a situation in which work is rejected or the client is disappointed, and the designer will be pivotal in ensuring that this does not occur. Communication is key to a productive working relationship with the client, and one of the most vital aspects of this in regard to commercial work is the programming and phasing of a project. Few companies or hotels, for example, can afford the luxury of completely vacating their premises and so any refurbishment would need to be carried out in carefully planned phases to allow the business to continue at the same time. Good computer systems, as well as digital cameras and internet transmission of data, facilitate this area of the designer's work, enabling the entire team to have access to work progress, as well as the means to update a schedule instantly and keep all those involved informed at every stage.

Employing an interior designer does not mean that clients are without ideas of their own – everyone is much more design-aware and informed these days – but it is the designer who can interpret these ideas and develop them through to a workable and professional result. A decorative scheme that a client may have seen in a magazine might look wonderful as it appeared in glossy photographs on the pages, but would be unlikely to work successfully if simply reproduced, in a dissimilar architectural setting with different orientation and light. It is part of a designer's role to interpret clients' needs and ideas carefully in order to guide them towards design solutions that will meet their requirements in an aesthetically pleasing and satisfactory way. A designer should not appear domineering or try to live out his or her own dreams at a client's expense.

For many interior designers, the most important thing of all is to try to exceed the client's expectations. Over the last thirty years, the priority for private clients has often been to obtain the cheapest quote, despite the fact that a home is probably the most expensive investment they will make in their lifetime. In this way, they have often put the cart before the horse, not understanding that quality design work costs money. The design industry is beginning to speak out more consistently and professionally on this matter.

The interior designer who creates a truly harmonious environment helps the client to be and feel different. The designer has an extremely responsible role, creating other people's homes and, in a way, making an impact on their destinies.
Tatiana Rogova (Russian) – designer

The brief

The process of gathering information from the client regarding requirements and lifestyle is usually referred to as 'taking the brief'. It cannot be overstressed how important this stage is, as without a real understanding of the client's needs, it is unlikely that a project will be brought to a successful conclusion. Consideration of lifestyle is all-important; what is the point of using up valuable space on a formal dining room, for example, if it is only going to be used two or three times a year and the client feels more comfortable entertaining in the kitchen anyhow?

With a private client, the designer will take time and care to establish what is required and to build up an accurate and detailed picture of the client's lifestyle. In some instances, establishing what the existing limitations are can be as crucial as establishing what the client ideally wants to end up with. It will be attention to detail that will help ensure a satisfactory result, one that will ultimately give the client what is needed in terms of storage, working space, comfortable seating and up-to-date technology, in a style they are happy with. Taking the brief is a logical process and some designers work with a prepared questionnaire to help establish the number of people in the household, how much time they spend at home, how and where they like to relax, eat, work, watch television, listen to music, cook and entertain. There might be an elderly relative living with the family, raising all sorts of safety and access considerations, or pets, necessitating a particularly practical approach to the final choice of materials and finishes.

The initial meeting with the client gives both parties the opportunity to get to know one another and form a view as to whether they would make a successful working partnership. If the client is unfamiliar with a designer's work then it would also provide a chance to browse through a portfolio. The designer can use the meeting to make an initial assessment of the site, and take note of the existing decoration, which may give valuable clues to the client's taste, style and the way they live.

Occasionally, a designer will have grave reservations about working with particular clients or being able to meet their requirements and, in that instance, it is advisable to decline the work politely or recommend another designer. Many designers opt to make a preliminary visit, for which there is no charge, before the full briefing meeting in order to establish whether the relationship will work.

A commercial brief will need to take into account market factors, branding and particular considerations applicable to the clients involved. It would also require the designer to take the time to talk in depth to key people working in the specific commercial area in order to understand exactly how the operation works and any particular requirements, constraints or practical considerations the proposed project might raise. Designing for public spaces can be extremely exciting and challenging and it is many people's dream to design restaurants, bars and boutique hotels. There is always a risk, however, with this type of work that some designers will be tempted to be too gimmicky and fashionable.

Although not always the easiest area to discuss, it will be important for the designer to get some idea from the clients of the budget that is available in order to come back with realistic design proposals for the circumstances. Inevitably, some clients may have very fixed ideas about their requirements which are not viable within the budget they are suggesting, while others are concerned about setting any form of budget figure for fear of the designer's reaction, or even derision. However, it is obviously an area that needs early agreement if the project is to reach a satisfactory conclusion (see chapter 5).

A key consideration for commercial projects is circulation. In Lupino, a multi-purpose venue in Barcelona, which includes café lounge, cocktail bar, restaurant and chill-out area, a dark-blue catwalk is used to guide customers through the different sections.

The survey

The survey is a vital part of the fact-gathering operation and breaks down into two parts.

Firstly, the space needs to be measured so that scale drawings can be produced as a basis for the spatial planning and subsequent layout. This is then followed by a thorough analysis of the existing space. The detailed measurements of the space, which are taken by working systematically all the way around the site, are recorded on a rough floor plan of the area and would include any existing fitted furniture. It is important to allow enough space around the plan for the inclusion of dimensions. The designer would also mark in the position of any existing services such as a soil pipe, gas pipes, radiators or television, and electrical sockets and switches. Important details include the depth and height of any skirting boards, dados, dado rails, picture rails and cornices. Also added to the plan are the height of window sills from the floor as well as the depth and width of sills, window-frame reveals and architraves. As the traffic flow through the space could be affected by the swings of windows and doors (including those on cupboards), these elements are also included in the measurements for a survey.

The orientation and resultant quality of light and strength of sunlight are likely to affect decisions on the design and decoration, and so the way a room faces would also be indicated on the survey plan.

The second part of the fact-finding process for the designer is to carry out an analysis of the existing space. This would include all the information pertaining to the space involved that is non-measurable. With the client's permission, the use of a video or digital camera can be a valuable additional aid to the survey process.

It is obviously important that the fabric of a building is in a decent state of repair. Older properties may have been built without a proper damp-proof course, for example, and there may be other hidden problems, which

Information gathered at the survey is a crucial part of the design process, allowing the designer to refer to the detail of the existing layouts and features of a space when working up new plans and schemes.

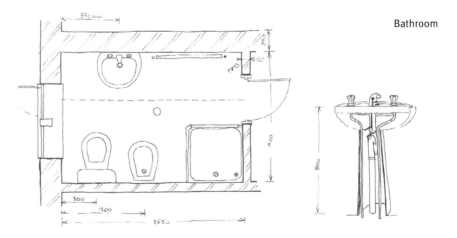

Bathroom

Top and bottom The designer needs to consider both the orientation and quality of light entering a room when planning a space. Most rooms benefit from some form of sunscreening or filter, even if decorative window treatments are not required. This living room (top) has fine, sheer screens fitted to the windows to reduce glare and provide some privacy. In rooms with skylights, such as the bedroom below, special types of blinds are available that can be manually or electronically operated.

obviously have to be remedied before any decorative work is carried out. Any such work would need to be built into the costings and schedule of a project. In some instances, existing problems may not be immediately obvious and the designer might need to bring in specialists to check a range of items such as roof timbers or floor joists.

To complete an analysis of a space for a domestic interior, a designer would provide a checklist for each room:

Ceiling

Does it have beautiful mouldings, cornices, a ceiling rose or other details worth retaining and restoring? Is it too high for the volume of the room? Are there unsightly bulkheads or beams that could be lost by introducing a suspended ceiling area?

Walls

Are they built of brick, stone, concrete, breeze or building block, traditional lath-and-plaster, modern plasterboard or timber studding? Is there any decorative plasterwork or panelling, dado or picture rails? Are the existing mouldings or panelling too restricting? What is the condition and style of the skirting boards?

Fireplace

Is the fire gas, electric, coal, log, solid fuel or smokeless gel without flue? If a gas fire is to be installed, is there a gas supply, or if a log/coal fire is required is there space to store the fuel? Does the fireplace need cleaning, restoration or replacement? A hollow-sounding panel on the chimney breast may conceal an excellent fireplace that has simply been blocked.

An existing fireplace may require cleaning or restoration. If the client requests a gas fire, the designer will need to establish whether there is an existing gas supply.

After measuring the overall length of a wall, the designer would take separate measurements along the wall, such as the corner to the fireplace, the width of the fireplace and each recess either side of the fireplace.

Survey measurements would include the width of a door and its architrave and the width of the area from the door architrave to the end of the wall.

Flooring

Does it suit the client's lifestyle and is it a practical choice for the function of the room? Is it a wooden suspended floor, concrete, stone or quarry-tiled? If carpeted, are there loose or squeaky boards, and what is the subfloor under the carpet? If there is an existing hard floor, does it need sanding?

Electrics

What is the position of fittings, switches and the quantity of sockets? What type of switches are there (for example, dimmer or dolly)? Do they need replacing? Where are the computer terminals, telephone and television aerial points situated?

Heating

Is the property heated by oil, gas, electric storage heaters, solid-fuel boiler with water-filled radiators, combination boiler or mega-flow system? Are there any existing radiators, or is there under-floor, warm-air heating or solar panels? Should radiators be boxed in or replaced for more efficient contemporary styles? Does the boiler need to be replaced and would an alternative form of supply or system be preferable? Are room thermostats positioned for maximum efficiency?

Joinery

What is the quality and adequacy of the storage already provided? What is the height of any existing joinery? Are there any kinds of new joinery, for example bookshelves, cupboards, radiator casings and other boxing-in, that might be required?

Doors

Are doors plain, flush, polished, painted, stained or in need of refurbishment? Maybe a plain flush door would be helped by the addition of a panel moulding? Are the architraves heavily moulded and worthy of attention? Does the door or doors bring you into the centre of the room, at one end or at one side? Does a door suggest a route into or through the room or would it be easier to work with if the door opened the other way? Would sliding doors be preferable? Is there an argument for enlarging the width of the doorways or raising their height?

Windows

Are the windows, or the views beyond, worthy of attention? Or are they difficult and unsightly and need screening, or even removing? Are there any trees in view and how will they affect the light and the view in summer and winter? What is the condition of the fittings and is there any double-glazing? Are the windows sympathetic to the architectural style of the room and how do they open? Would it be possible and appropriate to remove existing windows and replace with a folding glass wall?

Above In some countries, permission would never be given for the removal of fine windows in a 'listed' property, but some 'unlisted' properties might benefit from the installation of contemporary-style windows to allow increased light into the interior.

Top left When measuring windows, the height of the window-sill from the floor, as well as the depth and width of sills, frames, architraves and reveals, all need to be noted.

Left Consideration must be given to the style and quality of the panelling, decoration, positioning and architrave of a door.

Surveying a room

On a survey report, a designer should make a note of any existing furniture. A piece of furniture might be given a new lease of life if placed in a different room.

In a listed period building, planning permission will be required for the removal of specific interior decorative detailing, such as this plaster-work.

A designer should discuss with a client whether a fireplace is to be retained, restored or removed.

During the client briefing and when surveying the room, it is essential to consider any problems with circulation around a room in relation to its use and the client's lifestyle.

It is important to establish whether there is any existing storage and to explore where shelving or cupboard space could be installed, if required.

Note should be taken of any existing services, which could include radiators, electrical sockets, gas points or pipes.

It is essential to check what type of flooring is already laid, since it might be possible to restore an existing wood or stone floor.

Above An important aspect of a design survey is to see beyond the superficial 'clutter' in a room and establish whether traffic flow might be improved by repositioning doors or radiators.

Opposite The early twentieth-century interiors of the Dorchester Hotel in London were designed by Oliver Messel, a trained set designer, whose designs were highly theatrical and baroque in style. The recent refurbishments, including the hotel's revamped lobby, shown here, are clearly influenced by the original design but the style has been pared down to suit the simpler tastes of today.

Other considerations

If the room is already furnished, are there any doors opening back onto furniture or wall lights? Are there door stops to fall over? Is movement awkward around window openings or chairs and tables, including extra leaves that pull out? Is there an adequate variety of seating provided and where are the television, lighting and mirrors currently situated? Are there any trailing wires on view or are rubber grips needed under rugs for safety?

After collating all the necessary information in the form of the client brief and survey, the designer begins the process of formulating a creative response. To do this, a design analysis is written in which all the available facts and details about the client and the project are recorded. This forms a basis for producing ideas and concepts. Finally, a decision will then need to be made as to which are the best ideas and concepts to meet the brief and this would then be worked up to the presentation stage (see chapter 4).

An example of a wallpaper book showing a range of colour-coordinated patterns which could be used together or mixed with colours and patterns from other ranges.

Preliminary research

There is nearly always some element of research required in an interior design project. In the case of a hotel or restaurant, for example, a valuable part of the process of formulating ideas would be to visit other similar establishments to look at the space, the layout, the style and branding. Even for a residential project, some research may be required on the period of the architecture or a specific theme or style that the client has requested.

Nearly all projects require some research into materials and finishes and a design practice will have a trade reference library to help support this function. The content of the library will depend to some extent on the type of work undertaken by a particular practice but would be likely to include catalogues of companies supplying items such as lighting, furniture, glass and mirror, kitchen and bathroom equipment, suspended ceilings, partitioning, wallcoverings, floor coverings and accessories. In addition, there will be a range of pattern books and samples. Libraries are often set up to allow a designer to view a sample under both natural and artificial light.

Since trends and styles change so fast, many designers depend on the publications and seminars of market-research specialists, analysts and forecasters on a seasonal basis. Trade fairs and exhibitions are another important resource for the interior designer, offering for inspection the latest technology for interiors, new collections of furniture, materials, finishes and accessories, and inspirational room sets. It is usually possible to walk away from these events with a clear idea of what the major trends will be in the forthcoming months.

Many suppliers update their collections seasonally and a designer will make regular visits to their showrooms to see the latest products and discuss with sales representatives how these can best be used. Another source of new ideas and styles can be the show houses or flats that are put together to facilitate the sale of homes in new developments or apartment blocks.

A valuable part of a designer's work is to visit trade fairs and key exhibitions to stay abreast of the latest interior trends, styles and products.

Style considerations

Identifying a style that a client has in mind can prove difficult since style can often be a matter of interpretation or, indeed, misinterpretation. The client and designer might have very different views of what constitutes modern or classical style, for example. For this reason, some designers will ask the client to bring some magazine clippings to the briefing meeting that best evoke the look they wish to achieve. In some instances, clients will give very clear guidelines about style. However, if they are very open-minded or have no particular ideas of their own then there are a number of options open to the designer. One idea, for example, is to base the style of the project on the architectural style of the property, or in areas where the architectural features are not particularly dominant, there is always the opportunity to introduce an interpretation of a historical style such as Gothic, art deco or Shaker. Another approach is to work with a theme such as oriental, American colonial, industrial, romantic, retro or minimalist.

Of course, it is not simply a question of imitating a particular style, which would produce very sterile results. Rather, it is the inspiration of a chosen style interpreted through the individual approach of the designer to

Show houses tend to display the latest collections of furniture, materials and accessories, thereby offering the designer an insight into the styles and trends to come.

The original beams in the ceiling of this Mallorcan house make a strong design statement and impart a feeling of rusticity.

meet the specific brief of a client that produces a distinctive outcome. Minimalism, for example, may have endured as a popular international style but, as often happens when a style reaches high-street level, the look can often end up being all style and no substance. In recent times, a variety of alternative looks have evolved, all of which have in common the marriage of form and function. The concept of 'contemporary classic' provides a comfortable bridge between modern and traditional styles. These types of interiors usually combine contemporary furniture and design with luxurious and traditional fabrics. Colour combinations are simple and architectural detail is important and well-defined. Lighting is soft and diffused and window treatments simple and minimal with shutters or translucent blinds. Inspiration has also been sought from the 1930s with a look of sleek sophistication reminiscent of the great art deco hotel lobbies of the period. In this look, fabrics are sumptuous, colours are jewel-like, trimmings are lavish, surfaces are reflective and decorative objects are displayed *en masse*.

Formulating a concept

All designers have their own personal methods of accessing creativity in order to come up with a response to the client's brief. For some, the approach is to base the creative process on existing fact and work mainly with the design analysis. For example, a designer might ask a client to come up with three words to describe the sort of effect they want, such as 'light, elegant and

The conversion and renovation of an apartment in the historic centre of Barcelona by Enric Miralles and Benedetta Tagliabue combines contemporary furniture with distressed finishes in an imaginative play on the way in which historical styles modify interiors over time.

Above The sleek, elegant foyer of Claridges Hotel in London shimmers with reflective surfaces typical of the art deco period.

Left Minimalism, which was at its peak in the late 1990s, has now evolved into a comfortable marriage of form and function.

Concept boards

Concept boards help the designer move on from the methodology of the design process towards a creative response to the brief and provide useful parameters in which to work. Assembled in the same way as a collage, they tend to comprise magazine cuttings, photographs and sketches that evoke the style or theme of the intended design.

Above For this concept, the designer has picked up from the client a desire for warm, natural colours and the importance of a good, directional flow in the space. The use of materials will obviously be important in the scheme as will textural contrast, pattern (particularly curves) and reflective surfaces.

Right The designer expresses some of the potentially conflicting elements of the client's personality by depicting both warm and cool colours and textural contrast in a way that meets the brief, but still lends the scheme harmony and balance.

Contrasts of form and texture lie at the heart of this concept, with interesting ideas emerging around the use of shadow reflection. The images also suggest the client's love of travel.

The dynamic quality to this concept reflects the client's diverse tastes and interests. An image of urbanity is set against a desert scene, while a strong, industrial feel contrasts with suggestions of handcrafted elements.

welcoming'. Others may look for inspiration from natural elements indigenous to a particular property, perhaps picking up a handful of leaves, earth and stones from the garden and spreading these out on a table back in the studio to look at the colour and texture that result. Alternatively, the starting point might come directly from the facts gathered at the client briefing or from certain colours, shapes or finishes in a room, or a particular fabric, rug, painting or decorative object owned by the client. When seeking a concept, a designer obviously has to take into consideration limitations such as budget, the property itself, or lifestyle factors.

Some designers prefer to adopt a broad approach to the creative process, keeping a very open mind and staying acutely aware of everything around them. This can result in a more oblique, often more cerebral, concept emerging that is in some way related to the client's brief and that provides parameters within which the designer can comfortably develop ideas further. In commercial work, the name of a company or establishment might be the starting point for a designer's concept.

Some designers will formalize their concept into a board that they show to the client to evoke an initial feel for the design. Concept boards can successfully convey the essence of a design in a way that the more conventional presentation materials may not. They are usually put together lin the same way as a collage with an assembly of cuttings from brochures, newspapers, magazines, photographs and sketches that convey the style or theme the designer has in mind. Images and different colour combinations can be taken from a variety of sources, with garden, fashion or food-related images being just as inspirational as those with an obvious interior design bent. Taking inspiration from something other than an interior design magazine or brochure has the advantage of forcing the designer to stretch the imagination. A simple combination of colours or shapes, or the line of a dress can plant the seed of an idea which is likely to result in something far more original and inspiring than the replication of an existing interior. These boards can also incorporate interesting textural items such as paper, fabric samples or leaves.

Sketching up ideas

Once the basic concept has been established it will require further development and refinement. For the very preliminary ideas, there is no substitute for sketching. While not every interior designer is necessarily a fine artist, a sketch, however crude it might be, will help to visualize how a design idea might look within a space and whether it is worth working up further. These sketches might take the form of freehand perspectives or rough layouts which can then be worked up on tracing paper, or thin layout paper, over the original survey drawing. One of the skills that sets the professional interior designer apart from the enthusiastic amateur is the ability to work three-dimensionally and to visualize how a particular design or style might look within a space.

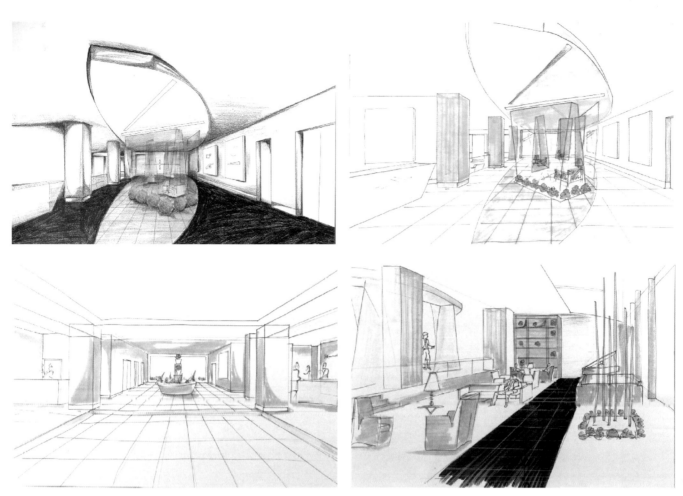

Moody perspective sketches convey the space and drama of this proposal for a hotel lobby.

Sketch-style elevations are used to illustrate details of the bar and window treatments and also the colour scheme of this small boutique hotel.

Bedroom

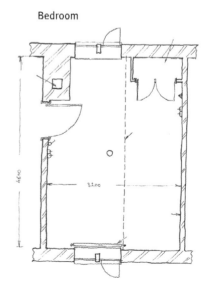

Sketches are an excellent way to record layouts.

Towards a design solution

Flexibility and an open mind are the keys to being able to develop a space in a way that maximizes its functional and aesthetic aspects. The creative and planning process can sometimes be a painful one and it can always be tempting to go with the first solution that comes to mind. However, it is important for a designer to keep pressing forward in order to come up with alternatives from which a more suitable solution might emerge.

There is so much to take into consideration to accommodate the activities that will take place within a particular space over and above the design basics of style, scale and proportion. Designers should also be aware of their responsibility for the environment, for example, and work with clients to design and specify in such a way as to create a healthy environment, making any future upgrades that might be required as easy and cost-effective as possible. In some countries, including the UK, there is only limited legislation in place to help protect the environment for the future. Building regulations may cover thermal efficiency but very little else. Interior designers have a real opportunity to contribute to our social and economic well-being by taking the initiative in this area and doing their research as thoroughly as possible. The word 'holistic' is bandied about in connection with designing interiors for the senses, which is a welcome development, but real holistic design involves considering any product specified from its acquisition and production through to its disposal, as well as ensuring that it is up to standard from an aesthetic and functional point of view.

Designers will always be needed for the perspective, balance and resources that they bring to each project.
Eric Cohler (American) – designer

Planning and design III

This chapter explores the principles of good design, how a designer integrates the complex services that the modern home, office or other commercial environment requires, and the different ways of communicating design ideas and solutions. One of the major recent changes in interior design work has been the need for designers to have a high degree of technical knowledge in order to accommodate the latest technologies in a given space and to liaise effectively with the various specialists involved.

The principles of design

The first part of any project involves the gathering and analysis of information as a foundation from which the designer can develop ideas (see chapter 2).

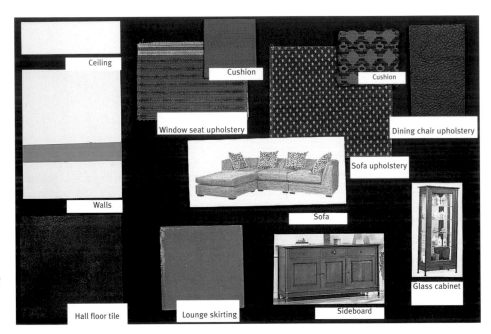

Ceiling

Cushion

Cushion

Window seat upholstery

Dining chair upholstery

Sofa upholstery

Walls

Sofa

Glass cabinet

Hall floor tile

Lounge skirting

Sideboard

Below and right The concept board provides the basis for the colour scheme. Here the colours have been successfully carried through from concept (below) to sample board (right).

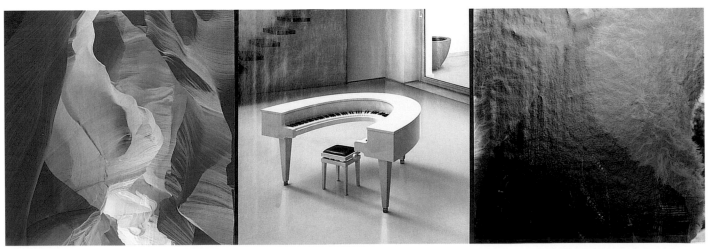

Innovative ergonomic design has done much to improve the working environment in the twenty-first-century office. This flexible space allows for 'hot-desking' and provides low seating areas for meetings and informal discussion.

The second stage is the creative one that, while largely intuitive, is guided by certain fundamental design principles and guidelines. There have been a number of such principles laid out over the centuries but their purpose has always been the same: to create balanced and harmonious spaces appropriate for their function. In order to achieve this end result the designer has to understand and consider the following key areas: human dimensions, scale and proportion, and ordering principles.

Human dimensions

It follows that to design spaces that are comfortable and functional for human use, a designer needs to understand human dimensions and body types. Human body types are divided into three areas – endo, ecto and meso. The identification and assessment of body types and how they are affected by age, exercise and environment is known as 'somatotyping', first introduced as a technique by W.J. Sheldon in 1940. The study of actual human body measurements and movements in a design situation is known as 'anthropometrics'. These studies allow a designer to take the size, shape and movements of the human body, including reach characteristics, into consideration to ensure that enough room is allowed within a space for people to function – stand, lie, sit, circulate – comfortably. A designer needs to be familiar with the amount of space that would realistically be required for certain activities in order to create spaces that are comfortable for the end-users. The amount of room needed for certain activities – putting a baby into a cot, shrugging on a coat, towel-drying after a shower or making a bed – as well as the most convenient height of a working surface or storage access all have to be considered at the initial planning stage of a project.

A further study of the perception and use of space involves the notion of personal space, or 'proxemics', and can differ from culture to culture. Its specific value to designers is in providing data on a range of social distances that are necessary for activities in the home, workplace and other public environments.

Form and function should be one.
Frank Lloyd Wright (American)
– architect

Greek classical style was based on a systematic use of proportion, embodied by Greek temples.

Scale and proportion

Scale represents the actual size of something in relation to a recognized standard while proportion refers to the relationships between the parts of a composition. Proportioning systems have been developed through time to try to establish an ideal measure of beauty. They have also allowed designers or architects to establish a consistent set of visual relationships that create balance and harmony. Our contemporary ideas about scale and proportion are still largely based on classical proportioning systems. The term 'classic' was originally applied to the higher echelons of Roman taxpayer and was gradually extended to encompass writers and the arts until its implication was one of 'a higher authority'. Historically, where there has been a return to classical style this has always been linked with a desire to return to law and order, perhaps recalling the splendour of ancient Rome.

Although the mention of classical style tends to bring to mind images of ornate architectural detailing, the fundamental basis of Greek classical style, which was based on the design of Greek temples, was all about proportion. What has happened over the passage of time is that the original detailing has been simplified considerably, but the proportions, despite being significantly scaled-down, have remained, and much of contemporary architecture and interior design continues to be founded on these same principles. It is these proportions that help a designer to plan spaces, work out layouts, and arrange furniture and objects in order to create a sense of harmony and balance. 'Ergonomics' (derived from *ergon*, the Greek word for 'work') is a study of the efficiency of persons in their living and working environment. It is the responsibility of the designer to ensure that any space designed adheres to ergonomic principles and that the resulting environment and products specified are comfortable, safe and efficient to use.

The golden section and the Fibonacci sequence

One of the earliest proportioning methods relied on the 'golden section', whereby a line is cut so that the smaller section is to the greater as the greater is to the whole (a relationship expressed in the 'golden ratio' 1:1.618). The golden section has always been a source of fascination for designers and architects and was known to the ancient Greeks and much revered by Renaissance theorists. Another method which achieved similar results, was developed by Fibonacci (real name Leonardo Pisaro), a thirteenth-century Italian mathematics teacher, theorist and philosopher. His highly influential 'Fibonacci sequence' was based on the following problem:

> *A man put a pair of rabbits in a place surrounded on all sides by a wall. How many pairs of rabbits can be produced from that pair in a year if it is supposed that every month each pair begets a new pair which from the second month becomes productive?*

The proportion between adjacent numbers in the series (after the first few) approaches the golden ratio: 1, 1, 2, 3, 5, 8, 13, 21, 34, 55… .

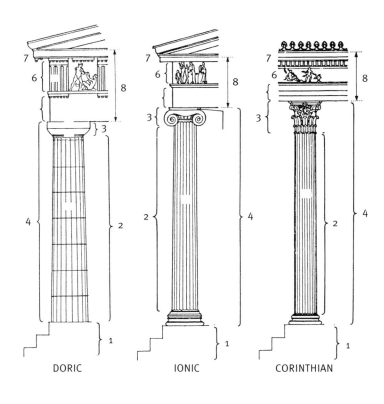

Key
1. steps
2. shaft
3. capital
4. column
5. architrave
6. frieze
7. cornice
8. entablature

DORIC   IONIC   CORINTHIAN

Above The symmetrical planning and harmonic principles used by sixteenth-century Italian architect Andrea Palladio have been a lasting influence on international architecture and interiors. Shown here is his Villa Rotunda in Vicenza, Italy.

Left The classical orders of architecture have informed the proportioning of western architecture and design through the centuries.

Classical orders

Perhaps the most major influence has been the 'classical orders', which in classical architecture were made up of a column with a base, shaft, capital and entablature, consisting of an architrave, frieze and cornice. These were decorated and proportioned according to one of the five types of order: Doric, Ionic, Corinthian, Tuscan and Composite.

There were two publications establishing the details of the classical orders. The first was by the Roman architect and theorist Vitruvius, who served under Julius Caesar, and wrote *De Architectura*, which ran to ten books and laid down guidelines for the design and proportioning of temples. Vitruvius' work was a huge influence from the early Renaissance on, after its rediscovery in 1414, with various editions and translations appearing in the fifteenth and sixteenth centuries. The second was a later publication by Italian architect Sebastiano Serlio in the sixteenth century, which provided the key inspiration for the Renaissance theorists in their work to restore ancient Roman standards and motifs. The great sixteenth-century Italian architect Andrea Palladio has always been regarded as crystallizing the Renaissance theories with his symmetrical planning, use of harmonic proportions and design principles related to art and the forms of nature.

Oriental proportions

This takes an entirely different approach to classical style, with its emphasis on symmetry and harmony, and is based instead on a simple grid taken from the traditional Japanese unit of length, the *ken*, a measurement based on a

The principles of design **69**

tatami mat, the size of which is roughly equivalent to the length of the human body lying down. In oriental-style interiors, ceilings are low and lines simple, resulting in spaces that feel more private and personal than those of the classical style. Oriental style is also more flexible than the classical, as there is no need to maintain a central axis and asymmetrical layouts are employed instead to create the required harmony and balance.

Le Modulor

A much more recent system known as *le Modulor* was put forward by the modernist architect Le Corbusier. It was based on the golden section and the Fibonacci sequence but worked in relation to the human body and was used to 'maintain the human scale everywhere'.

Ordering principles

Ordering principles provide a way of achieving a sense of visual order within a space. These include the following:

Datum

A line, plane or volume that provides a reference for the organization of forms and spaces into a pattern. Once a designer has established a fixed, horizontal line to work with, then all depths and heights can be established from that. When planning the furniture layout, a designer can then decide how the furniture can be arranged around the datum line.

Symmetry and asymmetry

In Greek classical architecture, spaces were given a strong line about which the various parts were systematically or symmetrically arranged. This axis, usually centrally placed, helps the designer create a sense of harmony and balance. Symmetry, which is sometimes referred to as 'mirror image' to help students grasp the concept, describes the balance of the distribution of equivalent forms and spaces around an axis or centre point.

A symmetrical arrangement is all about balance and form and generally involves working in pairs. As with all design principles, symmetry can apply to the vertical divisions of a room as well as to the horizontal ones. Symmetry is pleasing to the eye but can make a space seem sterile. A designer can counteract this by introducing small but deliberate touches of asymmetry.

Asymmetry, in contrast, refers to the balance of non-equivalent forms and relies on the visual weight of the objects, using the principle of leverage to balance their arrangement.

Radial balance for circular shapes is also an important design principle whereby in order to satisfy the eye, balance is required across the radius, as in the sections of a wigwam. If a designer were to place objects on a circular table, for example, just two might appear incongruous, but one large central one or several placed at equidistant points from the centre would look aesthetically pleasing.

Opposite A contemporary take on a Japanese bathroom with the square wood frames of the window and skylight based on the same grid pattern as a shoji screen and the square wooden basin and bath reminiscent of those found in a traditional Japanese space.

Right The use of grid patterns in this villa bedroom in Phuket, Thailand, imparts balance and harmony.

Below Although the classical style tends to be associated with specific architectural elements, such as columns, it is the designer's use of proportion that will determine whether a space feels harmonious.

Balance and contrast

In China, lines are traditionally believed to affect people psychologically. While horizontal lines create a feeling of tranquillity and vertical lines are more energizing, a combination of the two is said to bring about harmony. The art of feng shui stems from ancient Chinese philosophy and Taoist religion and is based on the belief that everything in the universe revolves round a cosmic life force known as *chi*. *Chi* itself is composed of the contrasting forces *yin* and *yang*, which should ideally be in balance at all times. Various adaptations of this ancient Chinese philosophy and way of life are now used throughout the world to create balanced and harmonious interiors. Although often complex, many feng shui principles can be related to Western ideas about ergonomics and the flow of spaces, and there are also parallels in terms of colour use, decoration and symbolism.

Contrast can be introduced into interiors in many different ways: for example, contrast of form whereby different shapes, heights and sizes are introduced into a space; contrast of colour (even the most monochrome scheme needs some point of contrast to sharpen it up); contrast of texture; and contrast of light and shade.

Rhythm and repetition

Too many disparate and disjointed elements in a space can be disquieting to the mind's eye and a designer can make use of rhythm and repetition of recurring elements or patterns to help avoid this. Ideas might include the regular spacing of identical objects along a linear path; a series of repeated architectural elements, such as columns or pilasters or a strong line of identical windows; or repetition of smaller details such as pictures with identical frames or decorative objects displayed in evenly spaced, dramatic groups.

Focal points

It is a natural human instinct to look for and be drawn to a fixed point within a space and however this is done, all rooms need some sort of focus or emphasis. This can be something as obvious as a fireplace or console table with an eye-catching display but could also be an asymmetrically placed focal point or something beyond the room itself that is designed to provide a frame for the view outside.

Internationally renowned designer Philippe Starck creates a sense of drama and rhythm at the Royalton Hotel in New York with the repeated placement of columns and feature light fittings and the regular positioning of chairs.

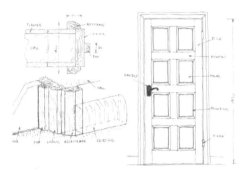

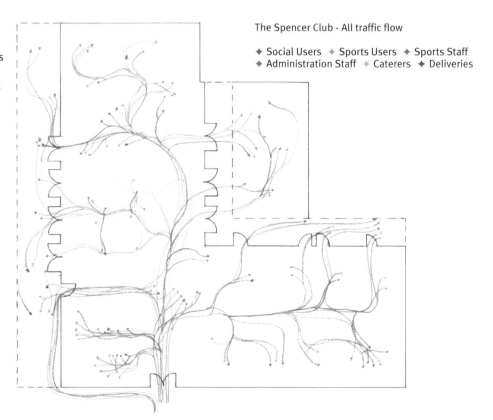

Above In order to make informed decisions about interior design and layouts, a designer needs to have a good understanding of how a building is constructed and be able to produce detailed sketches of key structural elements.

Right A traffic-flow plan helps the designer to ensure that there is a good circulation flow around a busy area. The various routes that users of a particular space are likely to take are mapped out, thus allowing the designer to check for potential bottlenecks and make any necessary adjustments.

Practical planning

Although a designer will always be aware of the aesthetics and holistic aspects of any space being planned, function and practicality are the other obvious priorities. An area must be designed and planned for a particular purpose or set of purposes and must cater for the needs and activities of the people occupying that space, with special attention given to any physically challenged users.

Circulation through a space is a crucial aspect of a design and a designer working on a restaurant, for example, might generate a traffic-flow plan to ensure that staff and guests can move about the space in comfort and safety, from entrance to tables, from kitchen to tables, from table to cloakrooms, and so on. In all planning, sufficient space needs to be allowed around furniture, and the opening of drawers, windows and cupboard doors or the positioning of door swings would all be considered as part of the process.

Storage plays a key part in all our lives and the designer has to plan this out with precision to ensure that everything required can be accommodated with maximum efficiency and ease of access.

Safety in interiors is also a planning priority and common sense dictates that a designer should take particular care where children or elderly people are concerned. The planning regulations for public areas are fairly clearly laid down, although they are still somewhat nebulous for domestic interiors.

The Spencer Club - All traffic flow

◆ Social Users ◆ Sports Users ◆ Sports Staff
◆ Administration Staff ◆ Caterers ◆ Deliveries

Structural considerations

Although most decisions that interior designers take on the structural side of a project would involve consultation with an architect, surveyor or engineer, it is obviously vital to have a good understanding of how a building is put together in order to assess the constraints and opportunities that present themselves, and to liaise knowledgeably with other professionals in the course of a project.

Playing with the rules

Flexibility is playing an increasingly important part in contemporary interiors and while there is much to be gained by opening up spaces to maximize light and living space, it is now understood that discreet and private areas are also sometimes needed within a home or working environment.

Sometimes a designer will look to separate an area of a large space without actually isolating it, through the careful placement of furniture or the installation of low or three-quarter-height walls with openings that allow light to filter through and communication to take place between the two areas. Spaces can be defined with floor and ceiling treatments and the oriental idea of incorporating moveable screens or sliding partitions has also recently found its way into Western interiors.

Above The central position of an over-scaled bath increases the perception of space in this refurbished period house by architect Eva Jiricna.

Left The introduction of screens allows for the flexible division of space. Here, a shower room and kitchen are accessed by a sliding screen.

Opposite top A glass floor illuminated from below is used to great effect in this cottage conversion in Sydney, Australia.

Opposite bottom Mirrors provide an obvious way for the interior designer to increase the sense of space and light and to distort scale.

Designers will employ visual tricks to increase the feeling of space or magnify small rooms. Removing or scaling down details such as cornices, which define corners and can sometimes appear to cramp the space, can expand the perceptions of space. Conversely, positioning one over-scaled piece of furniture in a small room can often increase the perception of space, since arrangements of smaller furniture, art and lamps can often be distracting to the eye.

Installing lightweight furniture or inserting glass panels in the floor further enhances space and light. A designer might also use lighting to soften the junctions between walls and ceilings or install a false back-lit wall that stops short of the ceiling for the same purpose. Height, too, can be amplified by opening up rooms or installing lanterns, roof lights or skylights.

Mirrors provide another tool that the designer can use to optimize the sense of space and light. In addition to hung, framed mirrors, large expanses of mirror can be installed between dado and cornice or adjacent windows, or above a chimney piece to reflect images and animate spaces.

For the designer who is well-versed in the principles of design, it is often a case of looking for ways to effectively blur the boundaries between traditional classical style and modernism or oriental style. So often, less is more, and the simpler the design, the more timeless and satisfying it is likely to prove.

Integrating the services

The services, though often unseen and perhaps not the most appealing part of the planning process, form a vital part of any interior space and have to be considered at the outset of a project. These services include heating, plumbing and drainage, lighting and electrics, air conditioning, security and integrated entertainment or communication systems. As there is no way that a designer could become and remain an expert in these fast-changing areas of technology, it would usually be necessary to work with specialist companies. However, in order to make design decisions and to communicate with specialists on site, the designer must ensure that they are as up-to-date and well-informed in these areas as possible.

The main services for buildings are governed by building regulations that give guidelines on the minimum standards required by a local authority. On completion, the local authority will inspect the installation to make sure these standards are met.

Heating

Common types of interior heating include central heating systems with oil, gas or solid-fuel boilers, and hot-water-filled radiators (usually combined with hot water supply for domestic use as well). Additionally, there are combination boilers and mega-flo systems, electric storage heaters, gas fires, solid-fuel fires, under-floor heating, warm-air heating, individual fires (electric, for example) and solar panels.

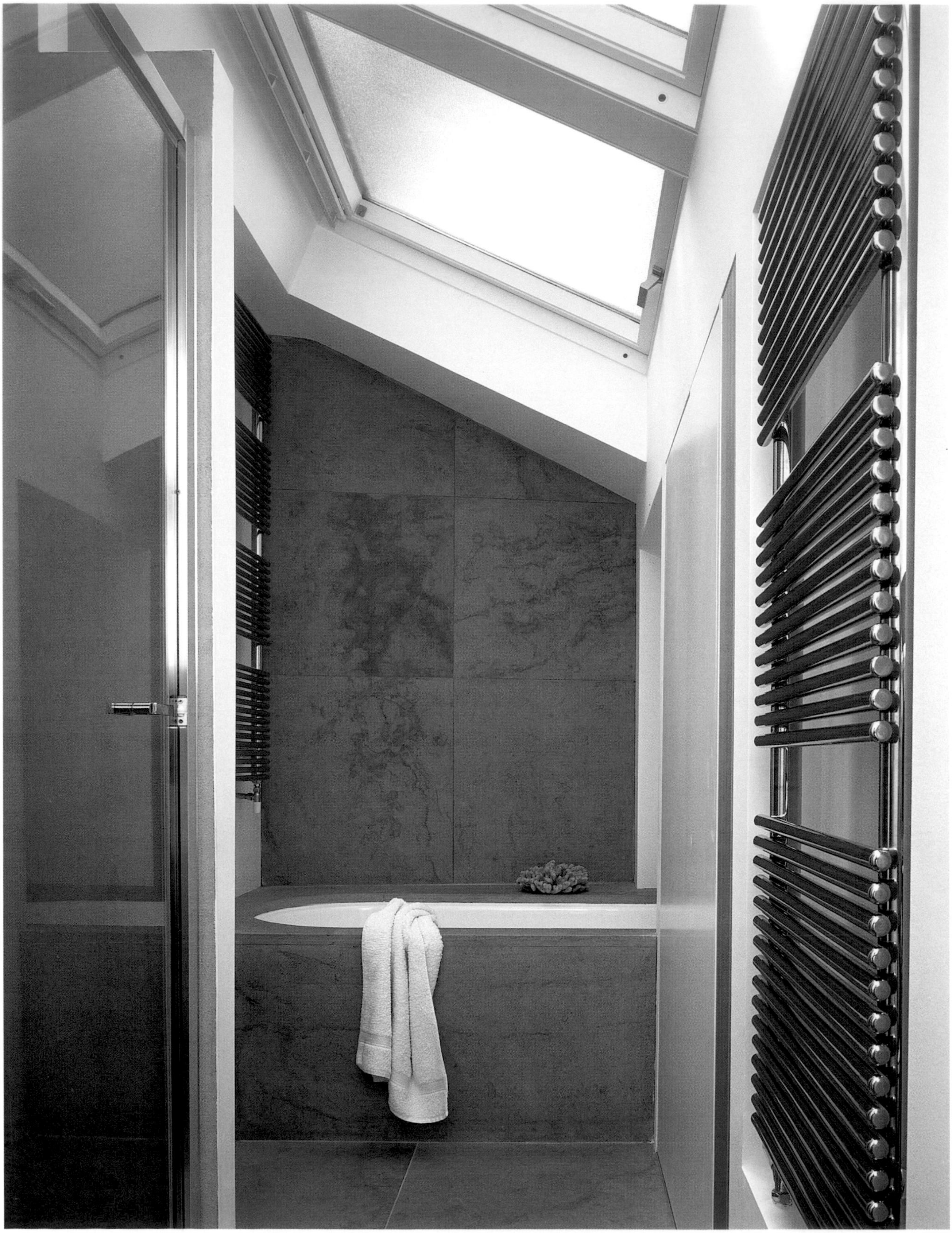

Interior heating is controlled by the boiler level, the room thermostat and the radiator thermostatic valve (if fitted) and the designer would need to position these for ease of access and efficiency of function but also so that they are visually discreet. In large projects the heating can be zoned with areas having independent thermostats to give an economic and flexible system.

Domestic water can be heated by a boiler with the back-up of an immersion heater but in small homes a combination boiler, where there is no hot water storage and the water is heated on demand, is also an option. In the UK, the conventional method of water distribution has been a gravity-fed system, where cold water is supplied to the property by a branch pipe off the mains supply in the street. This service pipe runs to the cold-water tank (usually positioned in the roof) and there is a branch of it that runs to the kitchen to provide drinking water. Pipes then run from the tank to serve the cold-water taps and another single pipe runs to the hot-water tank from where the heated water serves the hot taps. Water from the taps relies on the pressure generated by the position of the tank. The higher the tank, the greater the pressure, but this is sometimes inadequate for installations such as power showers which require the addition of a pump to boost the pressure.

This system is gradually being replaced by an unvented system where the water is again provided direct from the mains supply but the service pipes go directly to the taps under mains pressure, while water for heating is run to an unvented hot-water cylinder and the heated water is piped from there to the hot taps. There is no cold-water storage and, subsequently, all outlets are at mains water pressure. As unvented cylinders require building regulation approval and installation by qualified heating engineers thermal stores are sometimes used instead of cylinders. It is not possible to install power showers or pumps with this system.

In continental Europe and the US, the water is almost always supplied directly off the mains and gravity-fed systems are very rare.

Lighting

Good lighting can totally transform a space by energizing as well as illuminating it. The lighting should enhance the architectural style of a room, helping to create a specific ambience, and enabling the mood to be changed at the flick of a switch.

Installing new lighting often involves some structural work such as cutting holes in ceilings for downlighters or spotlights, channelling out walls, or cutting holes in woodwork to insert cables for computers or wall fittings. Installation would always be carried out by a professional electrician. However, while knowledgeable about installation, an electrician would not necessarily know much about lighting design and would need to be properly briefed by a designer and provided with a full specification for the works required and a detailed lighting plan.

As a general rule, functional fittings do the real work in a lighting scheme and decorative fittings add the style. The best solutions combine both,

Opposite While underfloor heating enables the designer to avoid incorporating radiators into a scheme, contemporary radiator designs can be introduced as features in their own right.

Light fittings

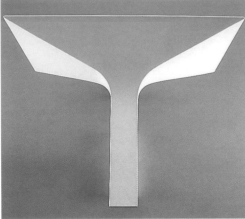

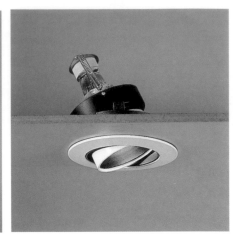

Bathroom lights such as this surface-mounted version need to be enclosed to comply with safety regulations. This fitting would be ideal on either side of a bathroom mirror and the frosted glass provides a soft light.

This contemporary wall-mounted mains-voltage halogen uplighter provides a good level of general light by bouncing light off the ceiling.

A fully recessed low-glare directional downlighter can be used for general or decorative lighting effects.

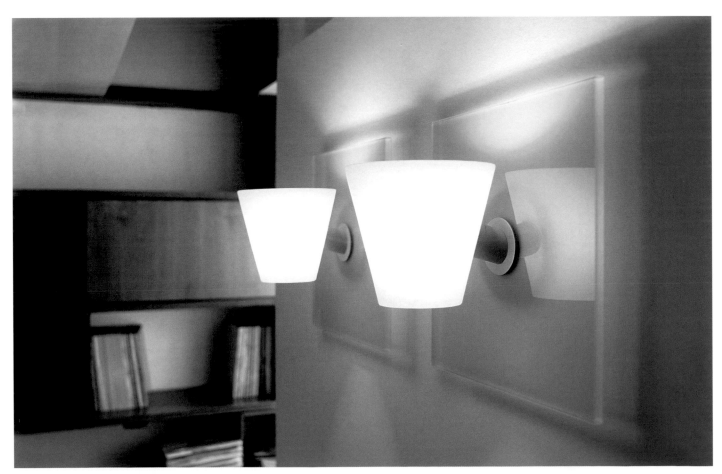

Wall-mounted uplighters provide a good all-round level of light.

Left Uplighting highlights the pilasters and cornicing of this shelving unit, while narrow beam downlighters cast light down through the glass shelves. The solid central shelves are illuminated with mains-voltage linear lights in a silicone strip.

A contemporary-styled surface spotlight.

A framing projector would be fully concealed and is an effective way to light pictures and art objects.

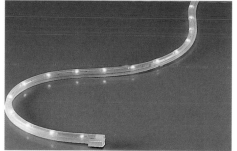

A miniature linear shelf light in a flexible, sealed, clear silicone is intended for general shelf lighting, concealed behind a profile, or for cornice lighting.

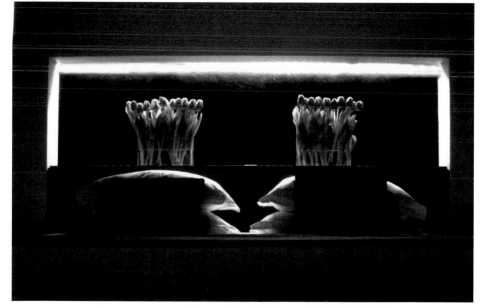

The recess behind the bed has been lit with low-voltage linear lighting to emphasize the niche. Mains-voltage linear lights are placed under the bed to make it appear as if it is floating.

Above Downlighters with a narrow beam have been directed onto decorative objects on the coffee table and on either side of the fireplace.

Right Recessed lights on either side of the stairs skim light across each tread. The golden doors have been downlit and the sculpture is lit by a framing projector.

giving flexible lighting ideas that adapt to changing requirements. When choosing fittings, the designer will need to consider function, size and appearance, flexibility (since the client's tastes and requirements may, in time, change), purchase and operating costs, and maintenance. To operate properly and efficiently, all fixtures should be cleaned regularly, and since all light bulbs (or lamps, as they are referred to in the industry) will need changing at some point, it makes sense to use long-life bulbs in places that are particularly inaccessible.

General lighting

This provides a good, all-round level of light – a blanket wash. For this purpose, a designer could use table or standard lamps, wall lights, recessed downlighters, wall-mounted or free-standing uplighters, wallwashers, pendants or chandeliers. Fittings should be in keeping with the style of the overall scheme and placed in such a way that there is no glare from the source of light. As a rule, pale surfaces make it easier to achieve good light distribution than dark ones.

A full lighting scheme would take account of the following three other elements:

Task lighting

This is needed for specific, localized functions: shaving, make-up application, bedtime reading, working at a desk, dining at a table, drinking at a bar and so forth. One solution is to use lamps that can be controlled to light the required surface. Track lighting with spotlights is versatile and easy to install – the spotlights can be angled wherever they are required. Other possibilities include recessed, low-voltage downlighters or fluorescents, which give a good, clear light but do need shading to avoid harshness.

Accent lighting

This is used to highlight pictures and collections, accentuate architectural features and add drama or create a mood. Directional downlighters or spots can be angled to illuminate a collection of favourite objects or sweep over interesting shapes or textures. There are many ways to light pictures, ranging from the picture light to the framing projector (a discreet ceiling-recessed fitting that beams directly onto a picture). Wallwashers can also make a room look wider by accentuating the walls. Also included in this sort of mood lighting would be flickering fire and candlelight, sometimes referred to as kinetic lighting. Fibre-optic lighting provides individual beams of light that travel down each fibre from a central light box. It gives a very precise light that emulates candlelight and is inexpensive to run.

Flexibility and control

The flexibility of a lighting scheme can be increased by using more than one electrical circuit, for example, table lamps on one (which would require lower-

When designing for the home office, the designer needs to integrate functional equipment into the scheme and deal with cable management and ergonomic challenges.

power lighting circuit sockets installed alongside the regular power points with switches by the doors so that lights can be switched on instantly when entering the room), wall-mounted fittings on another, ceiling-mounted or recessed lights on a third. A successful lighting scheme should have a variety of light sources that can then be adjusted to suit the function, mood or hour. Dimmer switches give maximum flexibility and there are now sophisticated dimming systems available that can also incorporate controls for sound systems, television and other technology. New technology has enabled lighting to be pre-programmed to individual settings to dim, brighten or change colour. Colour-change units allow the mood and function of a room to change at will – daylight simulation for reading or working, soft mood lighting for evening relaxation, and changes of wall or ceiling colour depending on the way they are lit.

Technological developments have also made it possible not only to have discreetly hidden central controls or small hand-held versions which will download music from the Internet or switch on the boiler, ventilation or security on request, but also remote-control operation, allowing the busy executive to switch on the heating, security lighting or draw the curtains from the remote location of a club-class aeroplane seat.

Services for communication

The advance of technology has had considerable impact on the work and role of the interior designer. With the pace of its advance, the designer has had to work to keep up to date with innovations in addition to the more traditional training. This continuing education is essential to equip the designer with the knowledge and sources to be able to solve the client's problems with the latest technology and to house this satisfactorily within an overall scheme. Advance planning is key to this, but it is also important that a designer understands their own limitations, referring to expert help when necessary.

Telephone lines are now needed for fax, e-mail and Internet access as well as for telephone handsets. Other high-speed data cables may also be required. Many people now work from home, connecting with their company through advanced communication channels. This is a specialist area and, while it would most probably be designed by a specialist, it is the designer who will need to integrate this functional equipment into the scheme, deal with the cable management and meet the ergonomic challenges.

Switching and security systems will be required in most environments and many clients request home cinemas with multiple speaker systems that involve specialized installation skills and careful acoustic consideration. So that television can be viewed in several different rooms, a designer would specify a multi-socket booster connected to the main aerial, and if satellite or cable television is also installed, each decoder unit would have a special aerial socket and power supply. Output from stereo systems is also no longer restricted to just one room. Music can be transmitted throughout the house and, although expensive, tailor-made systems are also available.

The home cinema is becoming increasingly popular and the designer needs to be aware of related technological developments and methods of installation.

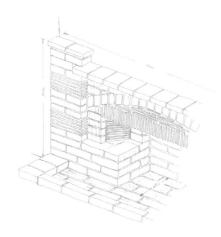

Above At the survey stage, the designer sketches key details, such as this fireplace.

Below A finished plan and section that have been inked and rendered, ready for presentation. It is good practice to have clear titling, including the names of the client and designer, on drawings.

Drawing up designs

Plans

Once the actual concept has been decided upon, the designer is ready to start drawing up floor plans to scale from the survey. A plan is a type of 'map' that is viewed from above and used to give an overall view of a given space. If a designer were to draw a plan on a scale of 1:1 this would indicate that the drawing is the same size as the actual subject; to draw up a room would require paper of the same size as the floor space. Clearly this is impractical and so a scale is chosen to fit a manageable size of paper. The most usual scale to work to for this purpose is 1:25 or 1:50 (in other words, twenty-five or fifty times smaller than the room). However, the number of drawings that need to be included on a particular sheet, the size of the sheet being used, and the amount of detail required would all influence the choice of scale. It would not look professional at the client presentation for a designer to show a plan that appeared cramped when mounted, and so the way that a plan is drawn up and laid out on the page will, to some extent, be dictated by the shape of the actual space involved.

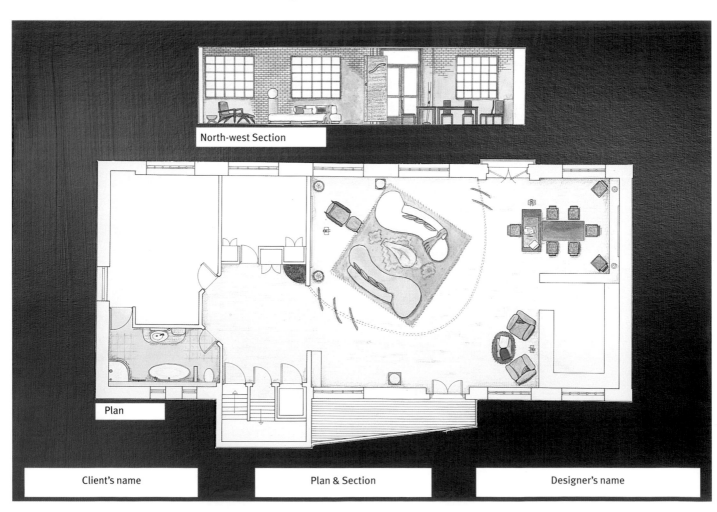

North-west Section

Plan

Client's name

Plan & Section

Designer's name

Early drawings are done in pencil and from this the final presentation plan is traced off in ink and copied onto detail paper or higher-quality paper if it is to be rendered and mounted on board. The plan in its basic form, ready for the progression of design ideas, would include the walls, showing their thicknesses and length; the openings of doors, cupboards and windows; the positioning of radiators; and details such as window-sills and skirting boards. There would also be a title block and an indication of the scale of the drawing and the position of the north point.

Sections and elevations

Since a plan is viewed from above, any changes in level or three-dimensional structures would have to be clearly indicated, which is why sections, elevations and construction detail drawings are sometimes necessary to provide additional information.

An elevation is a vertical plan of a wall – a scaled drawing showing a vertical view or detail of the design – and can be particularly helpful to clients who find the concept of scale on a plan difficult to grasp. A section shows how two separate areas divided by walls relate to one another and this is illustrated as a vertical slice through a wall giving a view of the interior space. It is usual to show at least two sections or elevations and to indicate on the plan where these are located. Rough versions of these can be used to try out problem-solving ideas and design solutions.

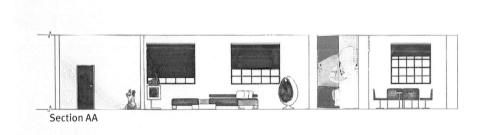

Section AA

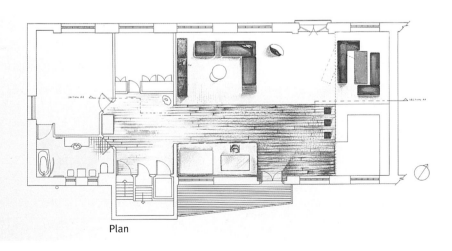

Plan

Elevations (vertical plans of the walls) are included with the plan and here show details of proposed window treatments.

The layout is initially worked out by moving scale templates around the plan until a satisfactory arrangement is achieved.

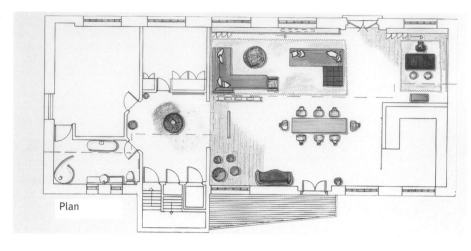

Plan

An example of a ready-made scale template that can be used for trying out different furniture layouts on a plan.

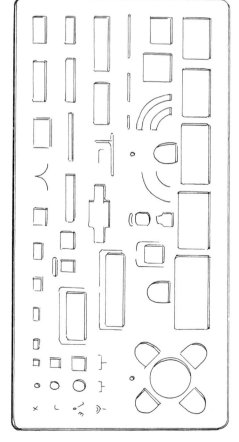

Furniture layouts

If there are to be structural changes to the space these would be considered at this stage, prior to developing the detailed furniture layout. In order to work up a satisfactory furniture layout, the designer will need to know the measurements of any existing furniture that the client wishes to use and will also have to source new furniture and then scale off from the dimensions of these. The designer would usually make templates of the intended furniture by taking the dimensions of each piece and then drawing to scale and cutting out the shape. It is also possible to buy stencil templates in a corresponding scale to the floor plan. These templates can then be moved around the plan until a workable result is achieved.

Contemporary product design and technology has provided the interior designer with many more options. For example, there are now modular elements for kitchens that can be arranged as wall-mounted or free-standing units. Each unit can be stretched and works with a sliding countertop system. The modules have an innovative ventilation system and everything including the kitchen sink can be hidden behind flush foldaway surfaces. Flueless gas fires have been developed that work without a catalytic converter so they can be placed virtually anywhere that has a gas supply. They can even be hung on a wall since they do not require a grate.

Graphics

Graphics are a fundamental part of the design and communication process. Graphic lettering, with a hierarchy of sizes to relate to the importance of the information, is used to identify each component or area of a drawing and for specific elements such as lighting and the services there are graphic symbols that have generally been adopted for the interior design profession. The repetition of graphic types and styles can give a presentation cohesion and, if chosen carefully to relate to a client or business or to suit a particular project, can help to underline or convey design concepts and solutions. Computers open up many more possibilities for graphics and text generated can be printed on paper or self-adhesive film.

Services and lighting plans

The services and lighting need be form part of the initial planning and design of a project so that they are fully integrated into the interior. Although almost anything is technically possible these days, major redesign of service entry points to a building can be very expensive, so the position of these may well influence decisions on the layout. If water inflow and soil outflow pipes are positioned so that they have the shortest possible runs to service appliances and sanitaryware, this would help to keep project costs down.

Services and lighting plans can be generated separately or shown as an overlay to the master plan, and the drawings are supported with symbols and a key. As the ceiling is not always the same shape and contour as the floor it is preferable to show the lighting plan as a reflected ceiling plan and include details and restrictions in the ceiling that would affect the installation or operation of the lighting. Services and lighting plans are either drawn in ink on tracing paper and transferred to acetate, or photocopied, or drawn directly on acetate with special pens. They can also be computer-generated.

Using computers

For the designer working with a full team of architects and engineers it will be essential to be able to produce all layouts and designs with a computer-aided design (CAD) programme. As technology improves, it will become very simple to project visual perspectives of anything, and probably in their correct colourings, which is a vital move forward. CAD is generally recognized as a very convenient tool for space-planning, presentation and communication and an immensely valuable labour-saving device. It also fits in with the contemporary way of communicating information, and no modern office could operate with it. However, CAD can be potentially dangerous if misused. If CAD is used in a project before the crucial details have been worked out, there is a risk of inaccuracy, since computer-generated drawings can quickly look slick and convincing even if all the crucial details are not in place. Using the special computer-aided design packages, it is all too easy to come up with seemingly plausible solutions that mask errors. Furthermore, a CAD-generated drawing can appear dull and uninspiring. CAD is not a design tool in itself and can never replace exploring an idea by sketching. Working up a design solution or a series of design options is fundamental to the notion of design as a problem-solving process. There is growing concern that not enough sketches are included in portfolios these days, since these can express students' ideas and thinking, as well as their emotional response to a design, in a way that CAD-generated drawings cannot.

After a solution has been decided upon, CAD can, of course, come into its own, especially as fine-tuning and the generation of additional drawings is easy once the master plan has been set up.

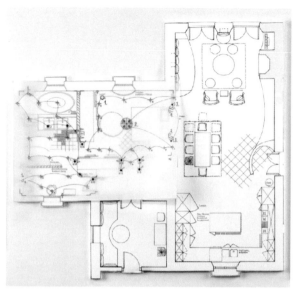

Above Lighting plans are often shown on an overlay – acetate or tracing paper – which can then be placed over the furniture layout.

Below Computer-generated drawings can be effectively colour-rendered and striking graphics for branding purposes can be carried through all the boards that the designer presents to the client.

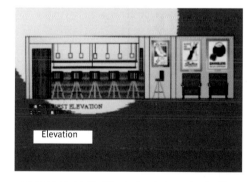

Elevation

Perspective

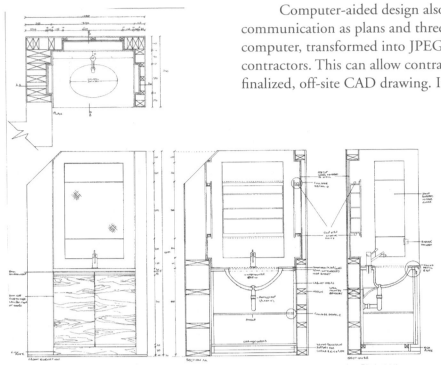

Detailed working drawings, such as these for a bathroom alcove, are produced to convey precise information to a contractor or planning officer.

Computer-aided design also greatly facilitates international design communication as plans and three-dimensional images can be created on a computer, transformed into JPEG files and emailed to clients, regulators or contractors. This can allow contractors to make furniture or fixtures from a finalized, off-site CAD drawing. It is not that unusual for a designer to have only one meeting with a client and then conduct all further business via email until the final handover and completion of a project.

The two main software packages that are used in the interior design world are AutoCAD, which is a fairly complex one often favoured by architects, and a simpler version known as MiniCAD. These can be used not only to produce two-dimensional plans, sections and elevations, but also three-dimensional drawings and even moving images that allow the designer to 'walk' the client through the space.

That said, many residential clients, and indeed some corporate ones, too, find CAD-generated illustrations too impersonal. Sometimes it is possible to get round this either by hand-rendering the CAD-generated drawing or by tracing off the visual from the CAD version and then rendering it for a much more 'hand-done' look – a process that is still quicker than drawing up a space entirely by hand.

Your eyes, skill and ability to deal with the real world is always more important than virtual reality.
Noriko Sawayama (Japanese) – designer

A particular difficulty for the designer is that it takes a considerable amount of time to absorb these new and fast- developing areas when there are so many other pressures on their time but there is no doubt that being able to work with computer-aided design is now an essential part of the designer's bag of skills.
Bill Bennette (South African) – designer

Working drawings

Detailed working drawings are produced after the client has agreed to go ahead with the project, in order to convey precise information to a contractor or planning officer on how something is to be constructed. These usually take the form of plans, elevations and sections drawn to scale and the drawings are functional rather than decorative and clearly annotated to clarify the designer's intentions or the materials and finishes that are to be used. They are often used for kitchens and bathrooms, details of built-in joinery such as cupboards or bookcases, or specially designed pieces of furniture, such as a reception desk or boardroom table.

Design illustration

Axonometric and isometric projections

To depict awkwardly shaped or angular spaces, two-dimensional, bird's-eye-view drawings such as axonometric or isometric projections are ideal, and lend a three-dimensional effect. They are relatively easy to construct, quick to generate and, despite presenting a slightly distorted view, easy for a client to understand. They are created by projecting up from the existing plan at an angle (an isometric does require the plan to be redrawn) and are particularly useful for kitchens and bathrooms.

Perspective drawings

These provide a realistic representational view where three-dimensional objects and spaces are shown by reducing their height as they become more distant. They can be a very effective addition to a presentation as they can capture the mood, atmosphere and style of a space as well as how the elements of a scheme work together and how they will look when the work is completed. An additional benefit is that there is the opportunity to personalize the illustration with details such as plants, paintings, a pet, or a view from a window.

Perspectives are based on a grid with either one or two points of reference depending on how wide an angle is to be illustrated. A one-point perspective is easier to execute but can look a little static, while the two-point version, where two lines converge towards two vanishing points is the most realistic and widely used.

In many practices, it would not be cost-effective to generate visuals in-house and the work is sent to freelance professional illustrators. Because of the time involved in producing illustration drawings, these would only be undertaken if the size and profit margin of a project justified the cost.

Freehand sketching

The same principles can be applied to freehand perspective sketching which can be a very attractive way of illustrating ideas for joinery, detailing, bed or window treatments to a client. They can also be produced spontaneously

Right An isometric projection allows for a bird's-eye view of the space.

Below This axonometric projection gives the client a very good impression of the designs for this large open-plan space.

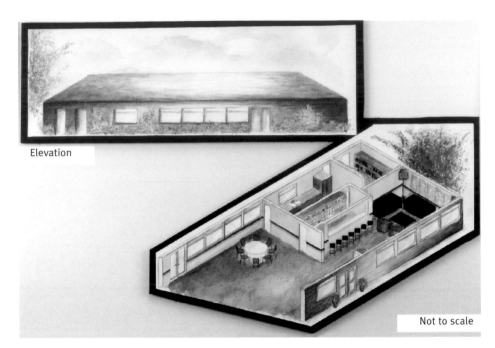

Elevation

Not to scale

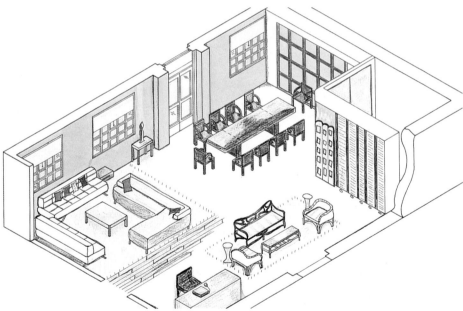

during discussions with the client where the client is finding something hard to visualize, or as part of the communication process for contractors and specialists involved. Freehand sketches can be equally useful to the designer in the early stages of a project to help visualize design ideas under consideration. Development sketches should also be kept along with more formal drawings.

Rendering techniques

These can be used to enhance a plan, elevation or section, making them easier for the client to understand by relating the colours to various elements of a scheme.

Below Freehand sketching is a wonderfully quick communication tool and helps the designer to visualize initial ideas.

There are various different mediums to choose from for rendering, but they need to be appropriate for the type of paper being used. Water-based mediums, for example, need paper that can absorb water (tracing paper, for example, would be unsuitable) and pencil crayons do not take on a shiny smooth surface. Watercolour is regarded as one of the most attractive forms of rendering and can be used to create myriad colours and subtle effects, while acrylics and pantone pens come in a huge range of colours and give an attractive contemporary look.

Marker pens are quick to work with and produce a distinct, bright result, while gouache – opaque watercolour – has great vibrancy and strength of colour. Watercolour pencils can be used wet or dry, while over-working or cross-hatching with ordinary coloured pencils can produce a variety of effects. Pastels mix well with other mediums and can be used to add atmosphere to a visual but they can be messy to work with and need a spray fixative to avoid smudging.

Rendering illustrations

Rendered illustrations can help bring a design to life for the client. There are many mediums to choose from, including watercolour, acrylics, gouache, pantone pens, spray paints, pastels and pencil.

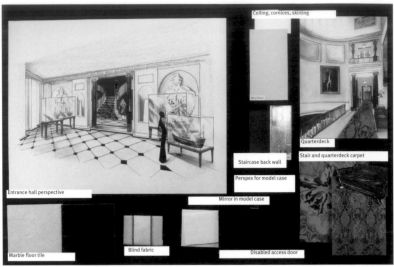

Above and right Mixed media helps add depth and texture to an illustration and enables a good replication of materials and finishes. These illustrations were produced using watercolour, pantone pens, spray paints, acetate and mirror card.

Above There is a light elegance about drawings rendered with watercolour and they are particularly suitable for traditional schemes.

Above Pantone pens were used to render these illustrations of banqueting rooms. Although the style of the decoration is traditional, the use of pantone introduces a contemporary edge to the presentation.

Left Different materials can be effectively rendered with pencil alone.

Harmonizing the elements IV

Once the spatial planning is in place, the designer will need to start sourcing materials, finishes, furniture and accessories and then develop a decorative scheme for the project. Colour is a key consideration at this stage and this chapter examines both the theory and psychological aspects of colour. Professional interior designers often use sample boards to show clients how a scheme might look and these will need to be worked up to include any detailing and accessories. The actual client presentation requires careful thought and preparation to ensure that ideas are well-communicated and 'sold,' and these days a presentation can include moving image and sound in addition to the more traditional plans, boards and illustrations.

Colour

Colour is arguably the most exciting tool at the designer's disposal. It has the potential to communicate instant atmosphere and style, and to create visual illusions. It is also one of the first aspects of an interior that people will notice; they may not mention the actual colour scheme, but they will remark on how cosy, rich, inviting, cool, spacious, elegant or intimate a room seems – impressions directly created by the shades of colour used.

Luminous colour has been introduced into this contemporary interior by back-lighting the curved glass walls.

The colour wheel

The key starting point for understanding colour is the colour wheel, invented by Sir Isaac Newton in 1666. Johannes Itten, who taught at the highly influential Bauhaus design school in the 1920s, developed it further and the colour wheel has subsequently become a standard tool in art and design education and for practising designers internationally. It is based on the three primary colours – red, yellow and blue – that are placed equidistantly on the wheel. The secondary colours between each primary colour are green, orange and violet and are produced by mixing equal amounts of the two bordering primary colours. If a third primary colour is added in an equal amount to its adjacent secondary colour then a tertiary colour is created (yellow-orange, red-orange, red-violet and so forth).

On one side of the wheel are the warm colours – red, orange, yellow – which are known as 'advancing' colours because they appear to come towards the onlooker. On the other side are cool or 'receding' colours: green, blue and violet. These aspects will help to define a colour's character in addition to its intensity.

Both warm and cool schemes will benefit from the introduction of sharp, contrasting hues to add life and sparkle to an interior. The colours that are opposite one other on the wheel are called complementary colours. These contrasting colours can be used as the basis for a highly stimulating colour scheme. For a more relaxing scheme, a designer would work with colours adjacent to one another on the wheel. This is known as a harmonious scheme, and can be warm or cool. In a two-tone colour scheme, it will be the intensity and proportions of the colours that determine which one dominates the scheme. A monochromatic scheme is where one basic colour is used but with changing value and intensity. This is quite complicated to execute successfully since there must be sufficient variance within the tones used and plenty of textural contrast to enliven the scheme. A designer can also opt to work with a triadic scheme that uses three equidistant colours on the wheel or even juggle with four equidistant colours which is known as a tetrad scheme.

The neutrals

A vast family of tints, tones and shades can be created from the primary and secondary colours by adding white (which produces a tint), grey (which results in a tone) or black (which is known as a shade). Another important group of colours – which does not appear on the colour wheel – is the neutrals. The only 'true' neutrals are black, white and grey. (Grey can be made by mixing black and white together or, more surprisingly, by mixing all the primary colours together in equal parts.) The more 'accepted' neutrals come in an impressive variation of hues that ranges from cool greys through stone and ivory to warm honey, straw and camel, with tones extending from white, cream, putty, taupe and ochre to charcoal and chocolate. The designer can therefore opt for a cool or warm scheme to fit the required mood of the room and then vary tone for contrast and definition. Although generally calm,

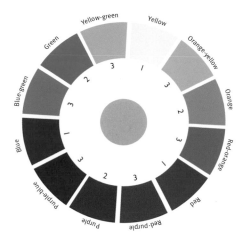

The colour wheel illustrates the relationships between colours and is a valuable tool to help the designer devise successful colour schemes.

Using colour to create mood

Architect Adolf Loos chose colours according to a room's function and specified bright, cheerful hues for the children's bedrooms in this house in Prague.

Fast-food restaurants, which depend on a rapid turnover of customers, often use primary colours to create environments that are too stimulating to linger in.

The fresh combination of apple green and white looks crisp and modern but also introduces a feeling of calm into the room.

Alvar Aalto selected yellow floors for the Paimio Sanatorium in Finland (1929–33) in order to express the healing powers of the sun.

Architect Seth Stein plays with space and emotions with the warm, soothing pink walls in this mews-house interior.

Neutral schemes are a versatile choice since they provide an excellent foil for pictures and decorative objects and can be instantly changed or updated with the introduction of toning or contrasting accessories.

sophisticated and relaxing, neutral schemes can sometimes appear bland or monotonous especially when applied to large expanses of wall and floor or large pieces of furniture. Touches of black and white can be a highly effective way of counteracting this as the white refreshes the neutrals and maximizes light, and the black gives points of anchorage and helps define surfaces that might otherwise appear to merge. A neutral scheme can also benefit from the introduction of a vibrant accent colour to give dramatic impact.

Colour psychology

With so much emphasis on the holistic side of interior design, the psychology of colour has been thrown into sharp focus and it is now well-understood that different colours affect the mind and emotions in a variety of ways. This is obviously something that designers should consider when deciding on a final scheme for a room or client. All colours form part of an electromagnetic spectrum and each colour vibration has its own wavelength which produces varying responses to which individuals react physically and emotionally. Red, for example, is the colour of vitality, energy and aggression. It is bright and exciting but can produce real physical reactions in the form of raised blood pressure or pulse rate. Blue, on the other hand, is the colour of peace, harmony and devotion but is also said to focus and sharpen the mind. It can be used to conjure up an impression of wide vistas and skies but, in some circumstances, can make the occupants of a space feel cold. Green is a harmonizing and healing colour and is regarded as a decorating classic for its versatility; in the same way that it provides the background for neutral earth tones and flowers of every hue in nature, green will team with almost any other colour. Yellow and orange are stimulating and energizing colours which are ideal for entertaining rooms, while soft pinks are soothing, and purples and lilacs add calm and spirituality to a room. Brighter pinks are said to spark passion. White over large areas reflects colour energies back into a room and, while hard to live with, will emphasize a feeling of light and space. If used as a bright accent, white can introduce an element of excitement. Black, by contrast, absorbs all colours and reflects nothing into a room and so can act as an energy barrier and make an area feel repressive. If a designer were seeking to create a rich, womb-like space, then brown, with its tints of red and yellow, would be a better option than black, as it would appear earthier and warmer.

The psychological aspect of colour can become particularly important in a commercial situation where it can be used in a manipulative way to create a certain environment. It may, for example, be used to prevent customers from staying too long in a fast-food restaurant or, conversely, specifically encourage customers to linger in a more formal restaurant. Colour can induce calm in potentially high-stress areas such as medical waiting rooms or can promote the retail process by guiding customers towards specific products in shop interiors.

Colour associations

There are many common associations with colour that can play a part in the design of a space: pink for a feminine scheme, for example, or white for purity and innocence. There are pitfalls here, however, since such associations can vary considerably from culture to culture. In the Christian religion, for example, red symbolizes the blood of Christ and martyrdom; it is the colour of cardinals' robes, and saints' days are written in red in the church calendar. For the Chinese, red is traditionally the colour of luck and happiness, yet for the American Indians and in Celtic lore, it is a colour associated with death and disaster.

Period colour

Since colour is also associated with different historical interior styles, a designer might need to carry out the necessary research when working on a period property, even if accurate reproduction of the original colours is not required. Neoclassical colours in eighteenth-century England, for example, included pale and medium greens, lilac, apricot, opal tints and a stronger range of blues, greens, pinks and terracotta, while among the colours associated with American colonial style at the same time were yellow ochre, blue-grey, ox-blood and deep blue-green, which was often teamed with burnt sienna. Although influenced by the English colours, the American pigments had more sheen than Georgian eggshell paints because they were mixed with milk. In France, the classical influence could be seen in the popularity of terracotta. Rich colours such as Pompeian red, chocolate brown, olive green, indigo, Prussian blue, burgundy and gold were fashionable throughout Europe in the nineteenth century, although it became *de riguer* in France to decorate rooms entirely in one colour, such as blue or green. Many manufacturers have now brought out specialist period-paint ranges that are invaluable for restoration or conservation work.

The perception of colour

Many factors can alter the way a colour actually looks when it is finally used in an interior. Light can make colours seem totally mismatched – even natural light at different times of the day can affect colour considerably. Such are the vagaries of light that shades that seem to match perfectly in one part of a room may look at odds in another part of the room. Indeed, it is not impossible for even wallpapers or fabrics carrying the same batch number to appear mismatched in different parts of a room due to variances in the quality of light, and if this occurs, it may be necessary to consider screening or filtering the light. Various types of light cause different colour rendition and so it is essential to check samples under all the lighting conditions in which they will be seen, both day and night. When there are light fittings that have a shade, samples should be viewed under the lamp as the light shining through

Above The elegant library at Kenwood House in England by Robert Adam is a fine example of neoclassical style. Neoclassical colour schemes were notable for their strength and vitality and the interesting combinations that designers used together, such as these striking blues and lilacs.

Opposite Vibrant green walls create impact and a complementary background for the display of prints in the entrance hall of Homewood House, Baltimore, Maryland.

the shade can totally alter the appearance of a colour. Clearly, a designer needs to consider the orientation of a room when putting together a colour scheme as well as the amount and quality of natural light entering the room. It is also worth considering that since the eye only perceives an object by the light it reflects, and the colour and quality of that light vary in different parts of the world, a colour scheme that would work satisfactorily in one country might not transfer well to another.

Colour trends are monitored carefully and there are publications and seminars available where specialists forecast forthcoming colour trends and combinations to help designers keep their schemes up-to-the-minute. It is also interesting to note that changes in fashion can affect the way colour is perceived, so that when staple colour ranges are viewed alongside newly fashionable ones they can appear totally different.

Developing a decorative scheme

When it comes to planning and developing a decorative scheme there will be a number of points for a designer to keep in mind. Plain colour schemes, for example, will need some textural contrast to create visual interest and depth,

The use of the strong primary colours blue and red for the furniture in this space is balanced by the bright yellow suspended ceiling.

and with a scheme involving a lot of hard finishes, this would have the additional advantage of helping to balance the acoustics.

The strength of a colour needs to relate to the size of the surface to which it is to be applied. For a bold scheme in a large room, the designer would probably use the stronger colours in the scheme on the larger surfaces in the room. To maintain a sense of balance in a smaller space, it might be preferable to opt for pale colours on the larger areas and limit the stronger colours to provide accents. Successful colour schemes are all about balance and strong colours need light relief, while sweeter, prettier colours benefit from counteracting with one or two smoky ones. Colour can be used to unify a room by painting all the woodwork in an identical hue, for example, and the wall and ceiling in a shade of that colour. Painting the woodwork a dark colour can lend definition to a space.

The sense of scale in a room can vary dramatically depending on the colour scheme chosen. Cool shades will impart an impression of space, while a strong colour applied to the lower stretch of wall below a dado rail will appear to reduce the height of the room by drawing the eye down. If the colour of the floor is continued up onto the skirting board, the room will look larger. The generally perceived wisdom for small spaces is to decorate them in pale colours to make them seem larger, although a designer might work instead to maximize the intimacy of the space by layering colour and texture to create an all-enveloping feel.

Walls colours

Curtain fabric

Chair fabric

Furniture wall sample

Flooring

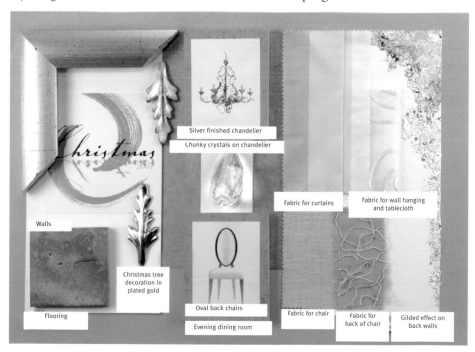

Silver finished chandelier

Chunky crystals on chandelier

Fabric for curtains

Fabric for wall hanging and tablecloth

Walls

Christmas tree decoration in plated gold

Flooring

Oval back chairs

Evening dining room

Fabric for chair

Fabric for back of chair

Gilded effect on back walls

Above A scheme that is limited to just plain colours can appear flat and lifeless but the addition of pattern and texture can revitalize it.

Left A palette of cool colours provides a simple way for the designer to give the impression of space in an interior.

Suppliers and trade accounts

Although there are good software packages available these days that a designer can use to help source materials, finishes, furniture, equipment and accessories, it is an important part of a designer's work to build up a trade reference library of high-quality, original supplies and then to establish good relationships with the suppliers (see chapter 2). The Internet is a useful way to track down potential suppliers, as are the various specialist trade publications.

If the designer is likely to deal with a particular company on a regular basis it makes good sense to open a trade account to obtain a full trade discount. In a one-off purchasing situation, the supplier concerned might be prepared to give the designer a discount if paid in advance. Opening a trade account can sometimes prove problematic, however, since the supplier may need convincing that the designer or practice is going to generate a certain level of business and this may be information that the designer can only supply once fully established. Most suppliers will want some detailed information about the designer or practice that is applying for the account plus accompanying references. Some will insist that the designer buys their range of sample books, which may be a substantial outlay.

Texture

Many schemes will seem insipid or lifeless if there is an insufficient amount of textural contrast and most will benefit from the inclusion of at least three different textures to add variety. Contrasting two very differently textured fabrics can immediately energize a scheme. Texture also affects the way a colour is perceived because of the way materials absorb and reflect light. Designers will often mix textures that reflect light, such as gloss

Most decorative schemes benefit from the inclusion of at least three different textures for variety and interest.

paint, glazed ceramic tiles, silky fabrics or highly polished furniture, with matt textures such as thick rugs or carpets, tweeds and linens, unpolished wood and matt paint to give a scheme life and interest. Textural contrast does not have to be limited to soft finishes, and layering hard textures such as frosted glass, richly grained wood and sleek stone can add depth to the most simple space.

Pattern

Pattern immediately introduces a style to a space but it can also be a practical choice since it can disguise marks that would be more easily visible on a plain surface. Pattern can also help to break up expanses of plain surface and add movement to a scheme. It can create visual illusions, with vertical patterns on walls lending an impression of height and horizontal ones making a ceiling seem lower. The designer needs to consider the scale of the pattern in relation to the space it is in and from where it will be viewed. Small patterns, for example, can take on a geometric effect when seen from a distance over a large space, while large patterns used in a confined space can be overwhelming. However, all rules are made to be broken and a confident and experienced designer can often handle different scales of pattern in unusual ways with dramatic results.

Pattern adds vitality to a scheme and provides the ideal way to break up an expanse of plain surface.

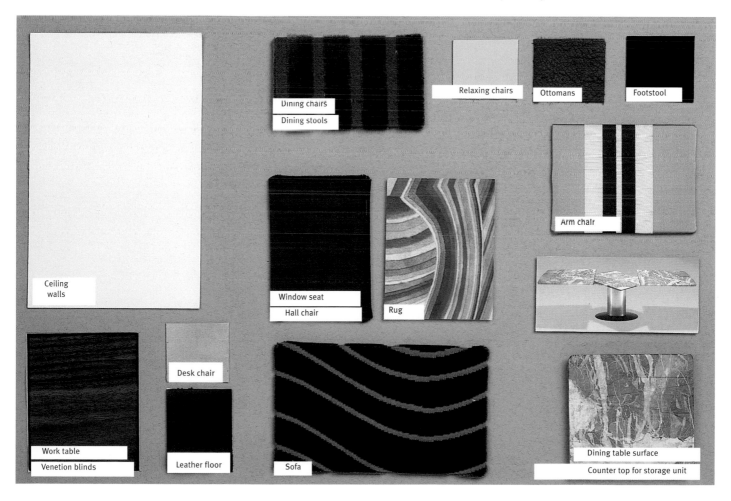

Ceiling walls

Dining chairs
Dining stools

Relaxing chairs

Ottomans

Footstool

Arm chair

Window seat
Hall chair

Rug

Desk chair

Work table
Venetion blinds

Leather floor

Sofa

Dining table surface
Counter top for storage unit

Above A terrazzo effect is achieved with irregularly shaped squares of glass paste in the Olivetti shop in St. Mark's Square, Venice.

Below The wide choice of hard finishes available today gives the designer great scope when it comes to choosing floor coverings and provides a simple way to introduce a feeling of quality into a scheme.

Materials and finishes

The wide range of materials currently available to the designer is both inspirational and daunting. Two of the most dominant areas in a room are the walls and the floor and so when choosing materials or finishes for these areas, image, style and practicality are all important considerations. As it is often hard to visualize how a pattern or colour will look, the designer would usually request returnable samples from the supplier instead of the smaller non-returnable swatches that could also be shown to the client at the presentation stage. Paints are available in small sample pots so that a colour can be tried out in the actual space and light where it is to be used.

The designer needs to be aware of laws regarding levels of fire-retardancy and in many countries furnishing fabrics are required to pass certain standards in domestic and commercial situations. It is the designer's responsibility to ensure that these regulations are met.

The right surface finish can help create the illusion of space or define an area. In a small home, for example, the same flooring used throughout will create an impression of greater size, while open-plan areas can be defined by a change in floor or wall treatment.

Floor treatments

There are three main types of flooring:

Hard flooring

This is usually permanent and an integral part of the building. Among traditional types of hard flooring are flagstones, terracotta, brick, marble, slate, granite, wood, terrazzo, ceramic and quarry tiles, while newer products include glass, concrete, reconstituted stone and even volcanic lava.

Resilient flooring

This is a semi-permanent option and is softer underfoot than hard flooring. It includes linoleum, cork, rubber, cushioned vinyl, thermoplastic, rigid and flexible vinyl, metal and leather.

Soft floor covering

This is normally laid on top of an underfelt or underlay, and includes carpet and rugs in numerous weaves, fibres or blends of fibres, as well as different widths. Natural flooring such as sisal, coir, rush and seagrass matting also come into this category. Many carpets are fully fitted, but contemporary or antique rugs laid over a hard flooring are another alternative and provide a good way to link or zone areas.

The choice of flooring is obviously influenced by practical and safety factors but needs to be considered as an integral part of the scheme. In fact, many designers choose to work from the floor up. Flooring is not always considered in decorative terms, yet large expanses often benefit from the addition of pattern or a border. It can also require brave handling, and wide planks for a hardwood floor, for example, give an interior more substance than the narrow variety. Unexpected materials can also be introduced into domestic interiors for impact, such as a woven industrial carpet, concrete or rubber flooring.

Pattern and borders incorporated into floor design provide an excellent way of defining and delineating space.

Right Many flooring companies now have sophisticated computer programs that allow designers to work up complex patterns and designs to order. This can be particularly effective in commercial situations, where designs may need to include company logos, or large areas of floor space need to be visually broken up.

Below The pronounced veining in the green marble on the walls of the main living room of the Müller House in Prague by Adolf Loos creates a feeling of continuous movement and makes a highly decorative feature.

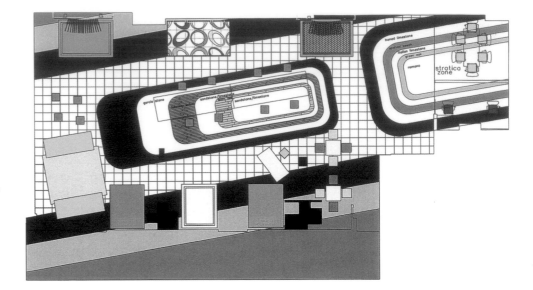

Many flooring manufacturers now have design studios equipped with CAD programmes to allow designers to adapt their ideas. Sometimes standard ranges can be made up in different fibres and colours or special designs, such as a company logo, can be incorporated into a carpet. Linoleum and vinyl can have inlaid patterns which may have to be cut on site or may be pre-cut by laser and then assembled on site. Flooring can be an expensive part of the overall budget as the necessary skilled installation is a high additional cost on top of the supply of the actual product.

Wall treatments

Permanent features for walls include ceramic, cork, metallic and mirror tiles, brick, glass bricks, laminated panels, polished plaster, wood cladding and panelling. There are two main types of paint: the water-based variety, which is used for walls and ceilings, and oil- or solvent-based paints for woodwork and metal. One of the latest developments in paint for woodwork is water-based gloss and eggshell finish. Other options include textured, metallic and spray paints or specialist techniques.

A single, large stencilled peacock feather makes an attractive decorative feature on the wall of this bedroom.

For wallpaper, there are many options other than the standard variety: flocked, embossed vinyl, woodchip, foamed polythene, metallic foil versions, sophisticated grass papers or paper-backed hessian. A luxurious effect can be created with fabric-covered walls. Contemporary developments include the dramatic repeat of hugely over-scaled individual designs, crisp graphic designs and exciting and vibrant overlaid combinations of colour.

Wallcoverings provide a way to introduce texture or pattern into an interior but decorative paint finishes such as dragging, marbling or wood

A simple gingham-checked Roman blind, a mix of patterns, and the casual arrangement of the duvet and quilt on the bed give this child's bedroom a look of comfortable informality.

graining, can also add interest and additional light reflection. Battening fabric onto walls or using paper-backed fabrics as an alternative to paint or wallpaper can give a space a feeling of luxury and intimacy with acoustic benefits, while fabric banners provide a way to soften the contours of a room. Stencilling or stamping can also be used to provide pattern and individualize an interior.

Wood panelling, panel frames of MDF or tongue-and-groove boarding can be applied to introduce a particular style to a room or manipulate the proportions. As with all the finishes in a decorative scheme, the interplay of texture and light will be a factor in the selection process and, when choosing wall finishes, the designer can opt for a stylish matt finish, a shiny, light-reflecting gloss or a silky mid-sheen effect. A designer will need to have a decent understanding of paints to be able to produce a detailed decorative specification.

Bed and window treatments

Even in the most pared-down interiors, bed and window treatments are crucial components of a scheme and a designer needs a good knowledge of fabrics in order to choose something that will give the necessary wear and hang. There is a vast range to choose from, including natural fibres (cotton, linen, silk and wool), man-made fibres (in which natural fibres have been regenerated and chemically treated to make them more practical) and synthetic fibres (acrylic, nylon and polyester), which were developed as a cheaper substitute for natural fibres. Woven fabrics can be very popular as they often provide the pattern and textural contrast needed in a scheme. The choice of fabric will of course depend on the style of treatment and the amount of light and privacy required.

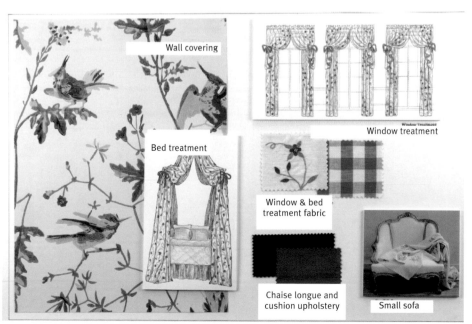

Wall covering

Bed treatment

Window treatment

Window & bed treatment fabric

Chaise longue and cushion upholstery

Small sofa

Left A traditional treatment, with a pretty, coordinated scheme for bed and windows.

Below A sleek, contemporary bed treatment with colour-coordinated headboard and valance.

Window treatments

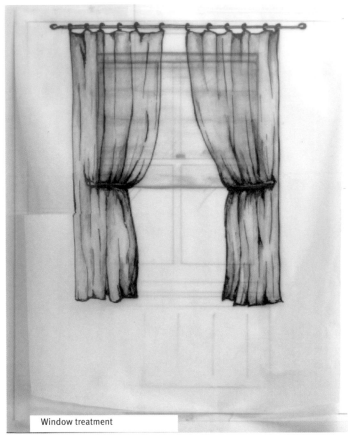

Window treatment

Textured fabrics and a metal holdback add interest to a simple design.

Face fabric – curtain

Fabric – roller blind

Curtain pole and holdback

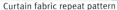

Curtain fabric repeat pattern

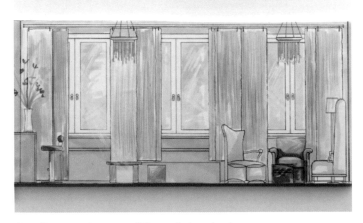

A continuous pole across all three windows lends this scheme a sleek, unfussy appearance.

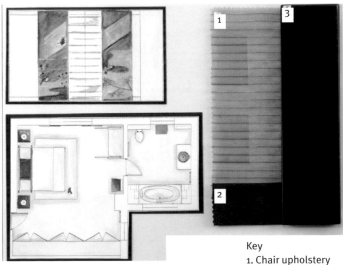

There are East Asian influences in this unusual window treatment featuring fabric-covered sliding shutters. Wooden slat blinds allow the amount of light entering the room to be controlled.

Key
1. Chair upholstery
2. Bathroom window sheers
3. Bedroom window shutter panels.

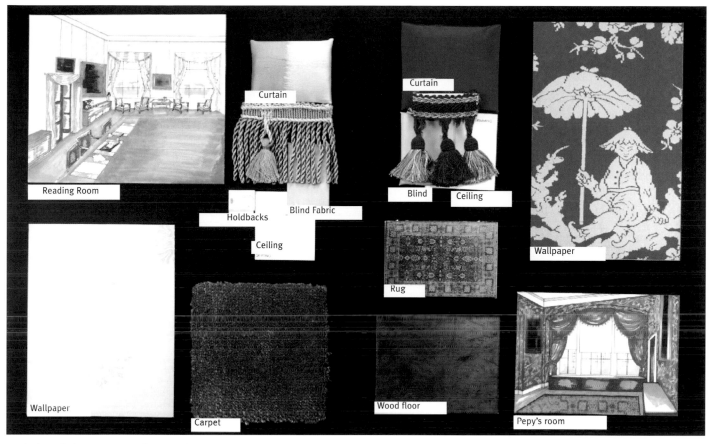

Reading Room

Curtain

Holdbacks

Blind Fabric

Ceiling

Curtain

Blind

Ceiling

Wallpaper

Wallpaper

Carpet

Rug

Wood floor

Pepy's room

Designing window treatments for period buildings allows great scope for using rich fabrics and lavish trimmings.

Face fabric

Pole and finial

Border fabric

Lining

Blind fabric and trim

A bobble fringe on the blind, a toile lining and checkered border fabric all lend originality to this scheme.

It is important that a designer understands how curtains are made and what styles will work in certain situations in order to produce practical and feasible designs for windows and detailed specifications for any curtain-maker involved. Blinds including Roman, wooden, roller and specialist varieties are often used to impart a feeling of simplicity in an interior. More traditional treatments and classic drapery, however, are still appropriate in certain situations and a designer needs to know where these will work and how to specify them. Headings for curtains and valances often dictate the overall character of a treatment and include pencil, French, box, tab, goblet pleat and smocking. Further choices include the type of suspension – track or pole – and the style and application of trimmings and borders should all be in keeping with the overall room scheme.

Bed hangings go in and out of fashion but allow great scope for decorative effect. Canopies can be as simple as a length of fabric draped over a short pole, or as dramatic as a full tester bed with accompanying draperies. Bedcovers, valances and headboards may all be part of a designer's remit and although fundamentally traditional in style, can be given a contemporary twist with natural materials, sheers, inventive trimmings and clean lines.

Clever designer touches can turn a bed or window treatment into something original and exciting whether it is the imaginative application of feathers, buttons or beads, the integration of antique textiles, or the provision of feet or castors in unusual woods or metals.

Selecting furniture

An integral part of any scheme is the selection of furniture and a designer can choose between free-standing designs or built-in furniture, which can be a good solution when space is at a premium. Solid furniture can be made in soft or hard wood, or MDF, block or ply, which can then be painted, laminated or given a spray finish. As with all design, it will be the attention to detail that sets a piece apart. A bespoke design makes the best use of space but can be an expensive option for a client since a good joiner or master carpenter will be required. The designer may need to generate working drawings for any special pieces required.

Mixing different woods in one room can be challenging and clients do not always understand that wood itself has a colour. The final choice of furniture will depend on its practicality in relation to the client's brief, its style, and whether it will fit and work satisfactorily in the actual space.

A subtle colour scheme helps to give cohesion to this design in which a number of different finishes have been used.

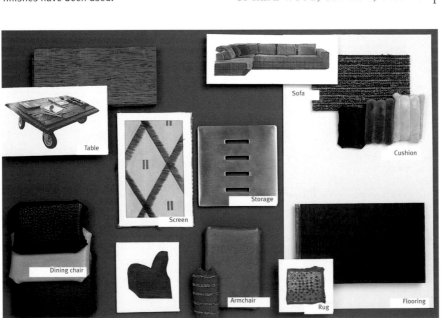

Table

Sofa

Screen

Storage

Cushion

Dining chair

Armchair

Rug

Flooring

Upholstered furniture

The type of upholstery, fabric and trimming a designer selects for a scheme will be largely influenced by practicality as well as style considerations. When the back of a chair or sofa is very prominent in a room the actual shape will be of particular importance since this can directly affect the style and mood of a room. Curved shapes, for example, tend to look more welcoming than straight and upright ones. The fabric that is used will also need to suit the shape and style of a piece and the actual positioning of a pattern also requires careful consideration.

Chairs and sofas can either have loose covers, which are removable and easy to change for cleaning or seasonal changes, or fitted covers which give a neater look and preserve the line of the furniture. The fitted variety are usually edged with braid or with spaced or close nailing. As part of the project planning, a designer will give careful thought to where furniture will be grouped in a space. Sofas and chairs should be arranged to create comfortable conversation areas and avoid leaving anyone isolated within a room unless, of course, a quiet reading or study area is required. As a general rule, designers try to avoid placing a large sofa across a window as it tends to block out light.

Clean, angular lines contribute to the contemporary feel of this bedroom in the Mann Residence in California. An ingenious and spacious storage unit combining a built-in window seat creates a particularly striking feature.

In the restaurant of the Musée d'Art Contemporain in Bordeaux, France, designer Andrée Putman uses a circular weaving as a spectacular wall hanging and focal point.

Details and accessories

Attention to detail is a key part of good design and a great deal of emphasis is placed on the way accessories are used in contemporary interiors. Details such as door and window furniture can appear incongruous if they are not in keeping with the overall scheme, while apparently modest additions such as stylish, good-quality handles can transform a simple piece of furniture. Accessories such as lamps, cushions, throws, rugs, vases, glassware and artefacts provide a way of pulling a scheme together and introducing texture, colour accents and contrasts – a modern painting hung over an antique console table, for example. The style of an object and the way it is displayed can give cohesion to a scheme and enliven a space with a touch of originality.

A designer may be closely involved with the purchase of artworks and decorative objects as well as items such as cushions, throws and runners. In a commercial situation, it is not unusual for a designer to specify even the smallest details, down to the flower arrangements.

Accessories can make or break a project. It is essential that the anonymity of a room is punctuated by personal objects.
Eric Cohler (American) – designer

Interiors have to be done meticulously to appear artless.
Kit Kemp (British) – designer and founder of Firmdale Hotels

Sample boards

Once the designer has decided on the different elements of the scheme and has pulled everything together satisfactorily, a sample board is produced to present to the client. A sample board is one of the most useful presentation tools since the different elements of the scheme are generally mounted in the same way as they would appear in the room – flooring samples at the base of

Choosing accessories

Attention to even the smallest details in an interior, such as the choice of door handles and knobs and the style and finish of hinges, makes all the difference to the success of a scheme.

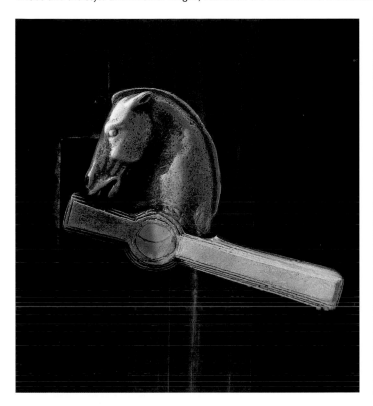

Creating a sample board

Minimum of 1 cm (1/2 in) border

Use neat lettering, lining up with the edges of the sample as far as possible

Cut the samples square and mount each one separately

Leave equal space at the sides and top of the samples

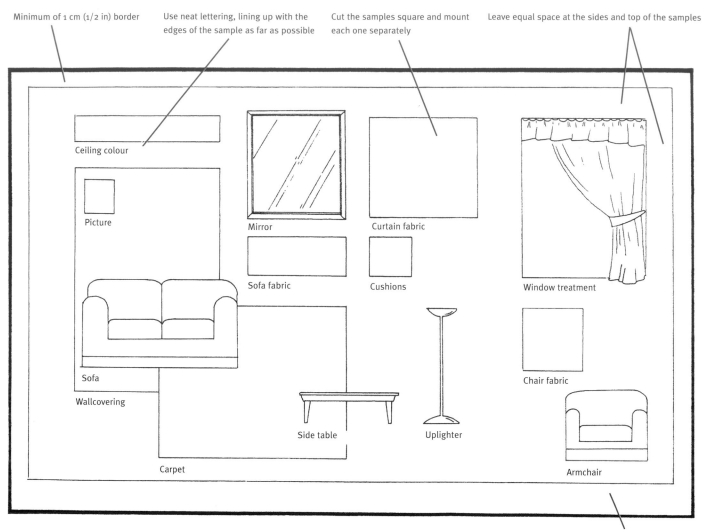

Ceiling colour

Picture

Mirror

Curtain fabric

Sofa fabric

Cushions

Window treatment

Sofa

Wallcovering

Side table

Uplighter

Chair fabric

Carpet

Armchair

Leave a wider margin at the bottom

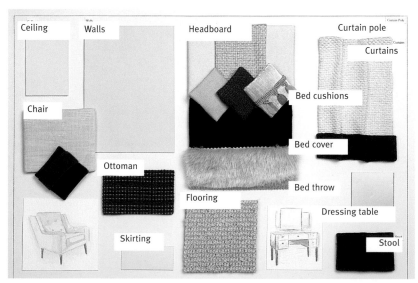

Ceiling

Walls

Headboard

Curtain pole

Curtains

Chair

Bed cushions

Ottoman

Bed cover

Flooring

Bed throw

Skirting

Dressing table

Stool

Above A sample board is a professional communication tool and, correctly laid out, will give the client a clear impression of a room scheme.

Left Touches of bright colour can energize and balance a calm neutral scheme.

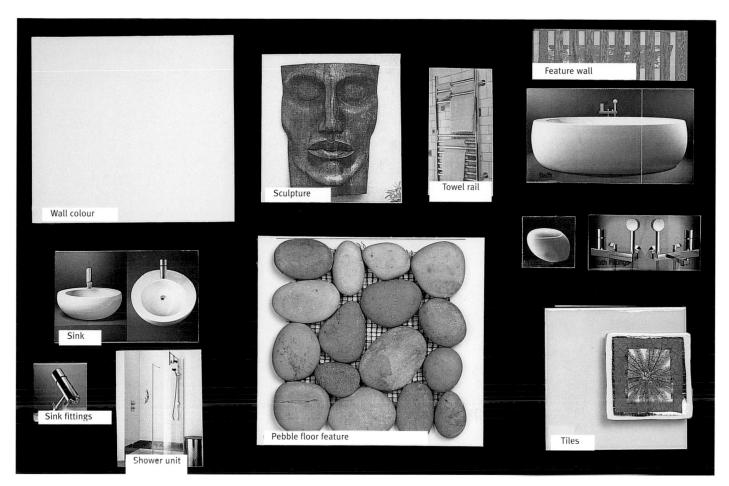

Ceiling and wall treatments are displayed at the top; flooring at the bottom.

Wall colour

Sculpture

Towel rail

Feature wall

Bath

Sink

Bath Fittings

Sink fittings

Shower unit

Pebble floor feature

Tiles

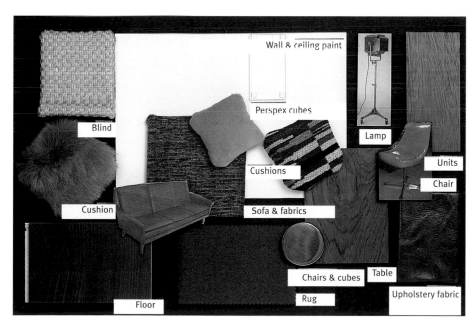

Wall & ceiling paint

Perspex cubes

Lamp

Blind

Units

Cushions

Chair

Cushion

Sofa & fabrics

Chairs & cubes   Table

Floor

Rug

Upholstery fabric

A sample board sometimes appears overcrowded if the furniture is included, and so a separate furniture board or an indexed furniture booklet is often presented to the client.

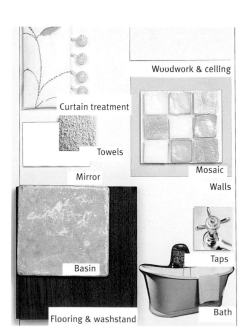

Woodwork & ceiling

Curtain treatment

Towels

Mosaic

Mirror

Walls

Basin

Taps

Flooring & washstand

Bath

A sample board for a bathroom showing finishes and fittings also conveys the overall style of the space.

the board, ceiling colour at the top – and in proportion to the way they will finally be used – small samples for cushions, a larger sample for the wallcovering, and so forth. It can therefore give the client an accurate impression of how the room will finally look. Assembling the sample board also gives the designer the opportunity to check that the whole scheme is working and to make last-minute adjustments where necessary. In some instances, there will be too many elements to include on one board, in which case the designer might elect to create a separate board for furniture or to devise a support booklet containing items such as accessories. If there is concern about how the client will react to a particular scheme, a designer may set up a pre-presentation meeting with the client to approve the selection of samples before they are attached to the board. In fact, some designers may not use a formal sample board at all for presentation purposes, preferring to show large, loose samples of the materials and finishes so that the client can get a really good idea of the look and feel of everything.

Preparing for the presentation

Presentations to the client may vary in style and degree of formality but the overall purpose remains the same: to communicate facts and ideas to the client. The size, type and extent of a presentation really need to be decided as soon as the design solutions have been finalized. Time-management is a factor here, since it would not make financial sense to spend a large amount of time on detailed visuals for a small project. The scale at which the plans are drawn up will depend to some extent on the shape of the space involved and the amount of detail to be shown. This, in turn, will affect the size of display board on which the plans are mounted for presentation and whether the sections and elevations are to be included on the same board.

The type of client would also influence the type of presentation since the requirements for a large corporate project, which might be attended by several directors of a company, might be very different to those for a small residential one where the designer might be just chatting through ideas with a client over a kitchen table.

A simple presentation for one area might consist of a floor plan and furniture layout with sections and/or elevations illustrating details of the scheme, such as proposed window treatments and built-in shelving, supported by a sample board showing proposed colours, materials, finishes, furniture, equipment and accessories. As already discussed (see chapter 2), some designers find it helpful to formalize their concept ideas on a board and show these to the client, too. If a full visual, such as an axonometric or perspective, is not appropriate for the project, then the presentation might still be supported by attractive thumbnail sketches to help bring the designer's ideas alive for the client. A keyed lighting plan might also be presented. For larger projects, presentation materials may include extensive rendered visuals. CAD packages are increasingly being used for client presentations, particularly where it is possible to visually walk the client through the space.

Project coordination and management V

These days, large projects tend to be run by project managers or quantity surveyors, who are specially trained to cope with the legalities and complexities involved. However, many interior designers still coordinate smaller projects, and this chapter provides an overview of the key stages and the related processes of a project, from start to finish.

Stages of a project

There are four main stages of an interior design project, beginning with the client's brief, the designer's proposal and the client's agreement to this proposal. The second stage involves gathering information on which to base a creative response and includes the presentation of designs to the client. Stage three, which follows when the client has agreed to and signed off the plans and designs, is when drawings are worked up in detail and all the pre-project preparation occurs. During the fourth stage, the works are carried out and completed and there is a formal handover to the client. These stages, along with the methods of charging or fee structure, would all be set out clearly for the client in the initial proposal, and the client would have the option to proceed with the designer through all the stages outlined or just one or two of them. A designer would usually charge for the briefing meeting but the client would not be committed to going on to further stages until they had agreed to the proposal put forward.

Stage one

The brief and design analysis

The first meetings with the client are not only to establish the nature of the brief but also to allow the designer to 'educate the client' so that they fully understand how the whole process works. Following increased interest in interior design in recent years, most clients tend to be well-informed about the subject and want to be much more involved in the process and so it is helpful to establish early on exactly how the designer-client partnership will work.

It always pays dividends if a designer takes the time after briefing sessions to write up a design analysis. This usually takes the form of a confirmation of the brief but would also include as much peripheral information and detail as possible. In essence, it is a way of managing information and creates a memory bank. This might seem an unnecessary measure for just one room but since most projects involve several rooms – a hotel, for example – and a designer might be involved in several projects at one time, its value can be clearly understood. The information collected here should help define the brief, give the client confidence and set out the fee structure. Attention to detail is of paramount importance; if the designer fails to note that a client has requested some particular and expensive repeated

detail, for example, which is not then included in the estimate later on, it could seriously jeopardize the client's confidence in the designer. The analysis should make decisions easier, helping to establish, for example, the client's expectations of a particular property – are they planning for ten years ahead or looking for a more short-term solution (see chapter 2).

Once the works have been completed there would usually be a formal handover to the client. The final invoice would be due at this stage, although the client might retain a sum for an agreed limited period in case any minor alterations or additions are required.

The proposal

The proposal should set out the various stages of the project, what the client can expect to receive in the way of drawings and illustrations, and a breakdown of project fees for services at each stage. In addition, it should contain detailed terms of business and conditions of engagement. A proposal should offer the client some flexibility and, in so far as is possible, be tailored to suit the client's requirements and schedule. There are situations when a designer should be prepared to negotiate and be sensitive to any possible constraints which could be related to timing, budget or legal or technical difficulties. In these situations, the designer could suggest alternative methods of approach such as phasing the work or looking at different fee structures to suit the project.

Although there are obvious advantages for a designer to see everything through from conception to completion, the client might prefer to work with the designer up to and including the presentation stage and then implement the designs themselves or with another professional. Another scenario might be that the designer is asked to work up the designs and carry out the pre-project preparation before handing over to a project manager.

Stage two
Surveying and measuring

Once the client has agreed to the proposal the designer can start the next stage of assembling information as a basis for the creative process, which begins with surveying and measuring on-site. A survey should always be as comprehensive as possible. A few extra hours spent on this at the beginning of a project will save days spent on-site checking details or taking supplementary information later on in the project. In addition to these practical tasks, time on-site can valuably be spent 'experiencing' the atmosphere and volume of

Obtaining accurate measurements of the spaces involved in a particular project and producing a survey report on the type and condition of existing architectural detail, such as a staircase and balustrade, is the next stage of the design process once the brief has been taken from the client.

space, which should help the designer in the overall creative process. This aspect is easily forgotten when concentrating on the survey itself and taking in all the meticulous details that will help define the space when it is drawn up (see chapter 2).

Creativity and concept

After taking and analyzing the brief and carrying out the survey and any initial research required, one of the most demanding and crucial stages for the designer is the creative process. Unfortunately, this is often one of the least practised and focused elements of a project. In order to access creativity, a designer needs to be totally relaxed and able virtually to daydream. When working to a variety of deadlines, this can be difficult to do and a designer can easily fall into the trap of adapting a tried-and-tested formula rather than trying to come up with something entirely new each time.

The creative stage usually breaks down into three phases. The first is to decide on a concept. This requires a completely open mind and the ability to think laterally. For some people, exercise and fresh air will help the process; for others, it will be a glass of wine and the gentle strains of classical music. Inspiration can come from a variety of sources. A concept may be based on key words picked up at the briefing session with the client, words of association, or a combination of imaginative ideas combined with interesting colours and textures. Taste, smell, sounds and vision can all play a part in concept development and can help unlock the designer's database of memory and experience. In designing for a client, a designer is, in effect, designing an experience and the concept should provide the essence of the scheme and clarify the mood.

Once a concept has been decided on, it requires further analysis, detailing and evaluation. Finally, it can be actioned, either in the form of informal images that provide working parameters for the designer, or as a more formalized concept board to show to the client at the presentation stage (see chapter 2).

Inspiration for a creative response to a brief can come from a multitude of sources including naturalistic shapes and forms.

A designer will usually try out a number of different room and furniture layouts in rough before deciding on the most effective solutions and would then draw up (by hand or on computer) a master plan which would form the basis of all the other areas of planning to be completed for the project.

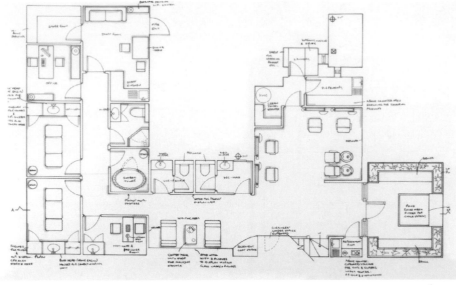

Basement plan

scale 1:50

Planning and design

A scale plan of the spaces relating to the project taken from the survey drawing and measurements forms the basis of the planning process and is supported by rough sketches to help the designer visualize how their ideas might look. Scale templates are used to help plot furniture layouts, although for larger projects this is often blocked out on computer. Once a final design solution has emerged the plans will be worked up for presentation to the client and supporting visual material prepared (see chapter 3).

The client presentation

Whatever form the presentation to the client takes, it is, above all, a communication exercise, an opportunity for the designer to show the client that they care about a project and to give the client confidence in their professional abilities. It should be a concise, focused, informative and human exercise.

Basic preparation for a presentation would include an analysis of the type of occasion and location and a profile of the actual audience. From this, the designer should be able to establish the formality, timing and approach of the presentation, as well as the appropriate dress code. The content and structure of the presentation itself is obviously vital and a designer would need to collect and select appropriate visual aids and material, and to structure the presentation so that there is an introduction, main section and conclusion. Presentation aids would be chosen to suit the location and to help reinforce the message, but would need to be prepared with care and used with skill. Too many or over-complicated aids may only serve to confuse the client and ultimately detract from the presentation.

Further useful preparation can involve deciding on whether to use full notes, brief notes as prompts, or no notes at all, and then to run through the

Presentation aids

Sketches of an exterior help to set the designs in context and illustrate any additional details suggested by the designer such as an awning, benches or planters.

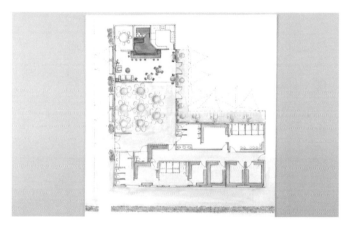

Rendering a plan, colour-matched to some of the suggested materials and finishes, makes it more accessible for the client.

Materials, finishes, furniture and accessories can all be mounted on a sample board.

It is sometimes difficult for a client to envisage exactly how a room will look from a floor plan and furniture layout; a perspective sketch, however, can bring the designs to life.

presentation a few times to help judge the timing, tighten up the content and reduce nerves. Spending a little time anticipating questions that might come up can also pay dividends. It is important to pitch the presentation correctly, too. The designer needs to show respect for the audience and retain the right degree of formality and professionalism for the occasion. Audibility, voice projection, enthusiasm and pace all go to ensuring a successful delivery, as does the appropriate body language, posture, and use of eye contact.

Client agreement

Sometimes a presentation will go so well that the designer feels euphoric afterwards, and on other occasions it may not be so successful. Whatever the outcome, it is important for the designer to remain focused on the next stage which is the closing of the sale. It may not be possible to get the designs signed off straight away but there are ways of encouraging the client through the decision-making process. Sometimes this will require some further work and adaptation, and it is important that a designer takes criticism positively, maintains a flexible outlook during a presentation and is not too fixed in their proposals. There are occasions when it is worth having alternative suggestions in mind, particularly in relation to budget.

A decorative specification ensures that there is no confusion about what is required of the painter/decorator and that the optimum quality of finish is achieved.

DECORATIVE SPECIFICATION

CLIENT: Silverman Productions Ltd
Silverman House
Battersea Wharf
London SW11

JOB NUMBER: MD/0084

BOARDROOM/EXECUTIVE DINING ROOM – Third Floor

CEILING: Paint ref: Dulux Brilliant WHITE One Coat, matt finish
WALLS: Paint ref: Crown 'FLAGON', flat matt emulsion
DADO RAILS: Paint ref: Dulux 'ICE STORY 3' OON 25/000, gloss finish
DADO: Wood Veneer 'LIGHT CHERRY' 4183, satin finish
WINDOWS: Window Frames – Paint ref: Dulux 'ICE STORM 3' OON 25/000, gloss finish
SKIRTING: Wood Veneer 'LIGHT CHERRRY' 4183, gloss finish
FLOOR: 'Maestro' carpet tiles – Colour ref: 200

General Notes:

- Decorator to prepare all surfaces for optimum finish
- All new woodwork and joinery to be knotted, filled, sanded down and primed
- Undercoat and topcoats to be applied following manufacturers' recommendation
- All existing painted woodwork to be washed, rubbed down, filled and sanded and one topcoat
- Existing wallcoverings to be stripped off – walls washed, cracks filled and sanded
- Decorator to use manufacturers' recommended adhesives where required
- No emulsion paint to be used as undercoat on woodwork
- Designer (or client) to approve all specially mixed paints or glazes on site before the specialist decorator commences work

Stage three

Implementation

Following the client's written agreement to the proposed plans and designs, the designer would collect information on all the products detailed in the design. Working drawings are then produced and these accompany the specifications and tender documents that are given to prospective builders, suppliers and specialists to provide a basis for them to prepare quotations. As it is important to ensure that clients understand every element of the design and its components, they would usually be copied in on these drawings.

Specifications

A great deal of time and effort is spent on specifying and pinning down the detail in a scheme and this part of the process can often take as long as the original planning and design. If, for example, a designer specifies a lamp, consideration needs to be given not only to the lamp itself, but to the type, size, colour and wattage of the bulbs; the size, shape, material and colour of the lampshade; the colour of the lampshade lining; and the colour of the flex. Accuracy is vital as mistakes or omissions are the designer's responsibility and can be costly. Samples of materials and finishes to be used can be included and a decorative specification would detail the colour and type of paint and the number of applications required. When selecting contractors, a designer obviously needs to consider their suitability in relation to the size of the project. If a contractor is new to the designer, it might be preferable to opt instead for a member of a professional association or to find someone who comes with a personal recommendation. On occasions, the client will also suggest contractors to tender.

A lighting plan is not always an essential part of the actual client presentation but it is a vital part of the specification for the electrician. The plan below illustrates the 18 different circuits and four varieties of light fitting in a proposed sports club.

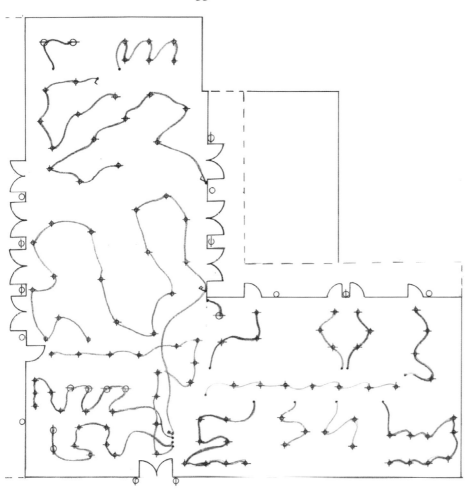

Key

+ Recessed downlighter
⊖ Downlighter
O External motion security light
φ External pillar light
⟋ One-way dimmer switch
⟋ Two-way dimmer switch

• Circuit 1 – Bar store
• Circuit 2 – Kitchen
• Circuit 3 – Bar
• Circuit 4 – Bar lounge
• Circuit 5 – Club house
• Circuit 6 – Disabled toilet
• Circuit 7 – Entrance corridor
• Circuit 8 – Female toilets
• Circuit 9 – Male toilets
• Circuit 10 – Locker room 1
• Circuit 11 – Locker room 2
• Circuit 12 – Locker room 3
• Circuit 14 – Locker room 4
• Circuit 15 – Female shower room
• Circuit 16 – Locker room 5
• Circuit 17 – Locker room 6
• Circuit 18 – Male shower room

Tenders and estimates

In most instances, contractors will be in a competitive tender situation or it may be a question of reaching agreement through negotiation. The cost and time involved in the preparation of an estimate for tender can be astronomical and so it can be very costly for a company if the outcome is not favourable.

There are differing views on the benefits of tendering. For example: 'Tendering allows the builder to take advantage of errors or misinterpretations in the drawings, specification, bill or otherwise' (James R. Knowles – contract advisor/adjudicator) and 'Competitive tenders selecting lowest price are adversarial to client and contractor relationship – lawyers benefit, quality suffers in order to secure work underpriced.' (Sir John Egan – extract from Egan report).

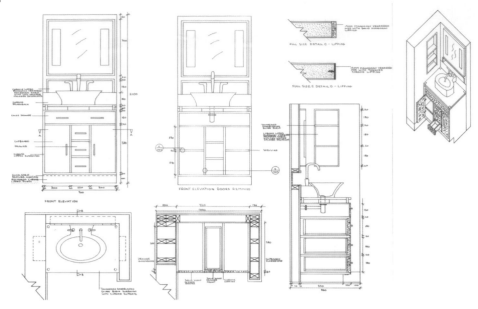

Working drawings, client estimates and contracts

For the selection of the main contractors it is usual for the designer to go through the tender estimates with the client and for the client to make the final selection, since the contract is likely to be between the contractor and the client rather than between the contractor and the designer. From the accepted quotations, the client estimates would then be prepared. A working drawing, as prepared for a contractor, is really a mini-design process in itself, requiring development, planning and design detail. This is where the fine detail is worked out – the lighting, the cabling, or the cooling system, for example (see chapter 3). Once this has all been sorted out satisfactorily then acceptance of contract would follow and the working drawing would become an instruction to the contractor. There are standard forms available for the purpose of contracting. The working drawings combined with specifications and contractor site visits would also allow contractors to prepare estimates that would form the basis of the client estimates.

Permissions and approvals

It would also be at this stage that the designer would seek any necessary permissions and approvals from the local authority. These should not be underrated as they can cause major delays and problems in relation to projects. The designer must be able to complete the necessary forms accurately and efficiently and should always follow up on all applications that might otherwise slip through the net.

The planning officer should always be consulted regarding changes in internal layouts or extensions or other changes to the exterior and to establish whether any proposed changes could be carried out under permitted development rights or whether further permissions will be required. This could depend on the volume of the property and size of the proposed development and whether there have been previous changes, additions and extensions made to the building.

In the early stages of a project, the designer might also need to consult with the fire officer regarding fire doors and escape routes. For commercial projects and public areas, permissions would have to be obtained not only from the fire officer but also the health officer. At the end of the project the planning officer inspects all the works and, if satisfied, issues the appropriate certificates. The district surveyor would oversee the progress of a project and the designer should check with the surveyor at key stages to avoid additional expense and delays if any work has to be redone.

Permitted development rights are also likely to be restricted if a building is listed or in a conservation area or an area of outstanding natural beauty. A listed building might only require 'listed building consent' but might also involve planning permission as well. Simple repair work may not require formal consent but a schedule of repairs would be drawn up and submitted to the local planning authority for written confirmation that the work may be carried out without formal consent.

Most countries have a national heritage body that looks after historic buildings and is under the control of an appropriate government department from which permissions for alterations or refurbishments would need to be sought. In the UK, for example, listed buildings are divided into three categories: Grade I, Grade II* and Grade II. The majority come under the third category as the first two are mainly for buildings of real historic merit. Listed buildings are not necessarily domestic; many theatres, cinemas, town halls, hospitals and so forth are also listed. Buildings in the US vary in grade depending on the type of business housed within the building in question.

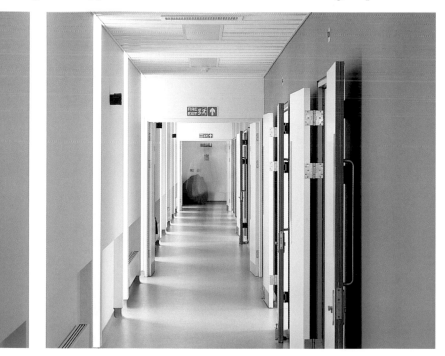

Many projects need the involvement of a fire officer to ensure the safety of people using the building. Fire doors, clear exit signs, fire detection and sprinkler systems, and emergency lighting are just some of the requirements for a commercial space.

This neat contemporary-style rear extension blends successfully with the traditional architecture of this terraced house and provides a light, spacious kitchen. Nearly all extensions require planning permission.

Stage four

Project management

There is often confusion about the difference between the management of a project and the overseeing of one. A designer may project manage (thereby becoming the project manager as well as the designer) or decide to hand over to a project manager. Courses of theory-based study and formal qualifications are available for high-level project management, but there are no rules or guidelines for simply overseeing a project. Most designers who oversee smaller assignments (usually defined as 'minor works') tend to learn on the job, often at their own expense or sometimes, regrettably, at the client's. In the US, there is more emphasis placed on project management in some interior design courses and therefore a higher percentage of interior designers do manage their own projects, regardless of size.

There is, of course, a world of difference between running a residential project and managing a commercial one. With the former, the designer is dealing with clients on a very personal level, whereas a commercial situation involves working with professionals, whether a committee or one individual. The commercial client will understand contracts and is likely to give a much more financially focused brief based on sales, marketing objectives and company image. It can be a valuable exercise for a designer to think seriously about which type of client they would be most suited to work with.

Responsibilities of the project manager

Overall, project managers are directly responsible for the success of the project. They are fully answerable to the client and should be aware of any risks involved. It falls to them to keep the momentum going, update the programme on a regular basis and negotiate any problems that arise. This will mean preparing and chairing regular meetings. On completion of a project the manager would evaluate the end product.

The project manager has an intimidating list of responsibilities which include the interior design of the project, the organization of the supply and installation of everything related to that design, instructing the contractor/s, the introduction of appropriate specialists, overseeing the implementation, reporting to the client and looking after the finances. Above all, the running and coordination of a successful project is all about good communication and teamwork and all team members should be involved and informed at every stage to ensure personal ownership of every detail of the project.

Schedule of works

One of the first things that the project manager would develop is a communication tree relating to the project team. This would be followed by the preparation of a job programme and schedule of works which needs to be set within a realistic time frame and schedule to ensure that the various

SCHEDULE OF WORKS

1.0 Demolition
1.1 Dismantlement and removal of any structures not required for the design.
1.2 Removal of existing wall coverings.
1.3 Removal of existing floorcovering and all the above from site.

2.0 Structure
2.1 Erect partition wall to kitchen area.
2.2 Install 5 panelled partition door track and hang doors, check level for carpet.
2.3 Check ceiling structure for suspended curvature light hanging, install wooden framework on concealed side of ceiling if necessary.
2.4 Fit wooden dado rail to height of 1m from level, as shown on plans.

3.0 Lighting
3.1 Fix suspended curvature light in position on ceiling.
3.2 Install spotlights and tube lights to suspended ceiling curvature light.
3.3 Mount mini starlights to ceiling as per lighting concepts.

4.0 Electrical
4.1 Install circuits as required
4.2 Fit dimmer switch to mini starlights.
4.3 Check all lights and socket switches are working.

5.0 Wallcoverings
5.1 Prepare all walls and window frames and woodwork for optimum finish
5.2 Undercoat as appropriate
5.3 Paint walls from ceiling to dado rail with 'Flagon', matt emulsion.
5.4 Paint window frames 'Ice Storm 3', gloss.
5.5 Paint dado rail 'Ice Storm 3', gloss.

6.0 Finishes
6.1 Install radiator casing.
6.2 Fit wood veneer to dado area as manufacturer's instructions.

7.0 Flooring
7.1 Lay underlay as manufacturer's instructions.
7.2 Fit carpet tiles as per plans
7.3 Clean carpet.

8.0 Furniture
8.1 Position table and chairs as per plans.
8.2 Polish and dust furniture if necessary.

A schedule of works sets out the stages of work to be carried out, including the demolition and structural stage, the installation of lighting and electrics, and the required surface finishes and arrangement of furniture.

contractors and suppliers are brought in at the right juncture and that reasonable time is allowed for sequencing, ordering and tendering, manufacturing, installation, and curing or drying. This programme would be updated monthly and everyone involved in the project would have a copy. Many large practices have a web-based project hub managed by the company that the various members of the project team, including the contactors, can access with a special code. Any changes would be automatically recorded and this information could be accessed by the project manager if required. Contractors and suppliers should always be seen as an integral part of the project team and good relations and communications here are just as important as the client relationship.

Preparation is also key to success and project managers should never allow a client to rush them into starting before everything has been properly scheduled and prepared. Lack of preparation can result in loss of quality and poor attention to detail.

Procurement

A procurement schedule is developed to ensure that materials, finishes, fittings, equipment and furniture are available for installation to fit in with the job programme. Placing orders requires accuracy and a designer will work hard to have a good rapport and working relationship with the suppliers to get the best possible help and service. If something is damaged on delivery, for example, a designer will want to be confident that the supplier will provide a replacement quickly. It will be important to establish a format for orders and payments and ensure that the client is happy and willing to sign any orders once the cost of all the items to be supplied has been confirmed.

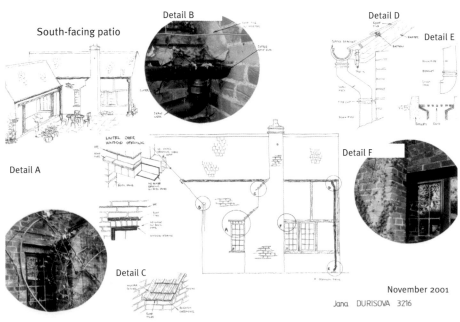

Successful site supervision is dependent on contractors being given accurate information beforehand. The detailed drawings of a house and patio shown here highlight the areas of the external building that require attention.

Site supervision

Site supervision is often an important element of the job even when a project manager is involved. Regular site meetings will be needed to discuss progress, any problems arising and any changes that might need to be made. These visits will provide an opportunity to check that goods have been delivered on time and that the cost, quality and schedules that have been set are being followed.

Since the main contractors are usually contracted to the client, there is always the risk of the client talking directly to the contractor and giving conflicting advice. Site supervision can be particularly difficult when clients are living on site, since they are often more in touch with progress than the designer and therefore more likely to be aware of a problem before the contractors can alert the designer. This situation makes it difficult for the designer to manage change and shield the client from inconvenience and upset. It can also increase the cost because of the hours that contractors have to spend clearing up at the end of a day. In order to avoid problems in this area, it helps to establish boundaries early on in the project to determine who is in overall control and how much input the client should have.

Construction design management (CDM)

Health and safety on site are important issues, and in certain circumstances a planning supervisor is required to oversee and keep records with a view to reducing risk and eliminating accidents. This does not usually apply to owner-occupier properties unless substantial demolition works are involved. Where a planning supervisor is not required, the designer should still undertake to recognize risk and to design with safety in mind, both for the duration of the works and for maintenance afterwards. In the UK, CDM applies if the works require demolition or the project is a commercial one that exceeds thirty man-days in work and/or more than 500 man-hours. Many contractors have a suitable contact such as an architect or surveyor who can fill this role and it is possible to gain a qualification as a planning supervisor.

Installation

Installation of joinery, materials, finishes and furniture has to be carefully planned, with consideration given to ease of access. The client will not be impressed when a delivery item fails to fit through a doorway. The overseeing designer or project manager should try to inspect each delivery and check for any damages. Delivery notes should be collected and invoices and payments noted. Constant liaison with contractors regarding the fixing of items to schedule will be required. Unfortunately, there are plenty of areas where a project can fail or fall short of the required standards. This can be due to late completion, poor-quality workmanship, lack of resources, lack of materials or if the work comes in over budget. A good designer or project manager will carefully measure the success of a project through client reaction, performance and reflection.

The refurbishment of a restaurant and bar

After the initial strip-out, the new services for the bar are installed.

The restaurant halfway through refurbishment.

Downlighting is installed in the ceiling in front of the bar area and is already functioning under the bar canopy.

The working area behind the bar is completed and equipped, ready for business.

Completion and handover

Just prior to the completion of a project a designer would carry out a thorough and detailed check on all the works, looking out for any damage to the paintwork, uneven flooring, poor curtain hang and so forth, so that these problems can be rectified before the formal handover. An advantage of the formal handover is that it often allows the designer the opportunity to impress the client. Many designers will hold back a sum in order to dress the site, perhaps with flowers, candles, chocolate and champagne and appropriate music playing when the client arrives. In some instances, a client may be absent throughout the project works and will ask the client to organize everything in the property right down to stocking the refrigerator. The design analysis should provide the designer with the necessary information about the client to do this successfully and to create the right design experience that is both pleasing and flattering to the client.

On the more practical side, completion would be accompanied by final invoice and stage payments and any guarantees, instruction or information booklets would be given to the client. This is generally appreciated by clients and it adds to the professionalism of the overall project if an after-sales maintenance manual is supplied containing everything to do with the work carried out, including items such as receipts, warranties, instructions, paint colours, audio/visual information and care of wood or stone flooring. It is usual for a retention period to be allowed, the duration of which would be

Clients always appreciate an after-sales maintenance manual detailing how to keep materials and finishes in good condition, how to operate appliances, and who to contact in case of technical problems. This can be particularly valuable in bathrooms and kitchens with finishes requiring special care, such as marble, granite, Corian, glass and stainless steel.

A designer can impress a client on completion of a project by dressing the finished interior with accessories such as stylish vases of flowers and bowls of fresh fruit.

agreed with the client at the contractual stage. Sometimes referred to as the 'snagging' or 'punch list' stage, this is where the client retains a small part of the fee while the designer would ensure that any post-project problems arising are satisfactorily dealt with. The period of time involved may vary from as little as two weeks to as long as six months, depending on the type of work involved.

Fees

Fee structures for interior design will vary depending on the complexity of the project but the following are the most usual methods of charging.

Consultant fee

For this, an hourly or daily rate would be charged and would be appropriate for the following:

- *A client who only requires a limited input from the designer*
- *Time spent locating artworks, antiques and other specialist items*
- *The first stage of a project before the definitive brief is completed*
- *A client who prefers to commission a designer on a time-rate with a set limit of hours agreed*

Combination of fee and mark-up

This is usually applied where projects mainly involve the supply of furnishings, fittings and equipment (FF&E). This could include a fee for the initial design concept and then any items supplied would be at a marked-up price (percentage on cost). In addition, a project coordination fee could be charged to cover installation of furniture, fittings and equipment if the job was particularly large or complex.

Fixed fee

This usually applies to projects with mainly design content, with or without the supply of goods. This could include:

◆ *A fixed fee to cover the initial design concept*
◆ *A fixed design fee to cover the development of the design up to a work-in-progress stage*
◆ *A project coordination fee (hourly rate or percentage of total cost of job) during work-in-progress stage*
◆ *An administration or handling charge*

Retail charging

In some instances, it may be appropriate to supply everything at retail cost in which case no other fees are applicable. However, retail charging can be combined with a consultant fee. Whatever the method of charging, the fee should be agreed with the client at an early stage.

Sometimes it is appropriate to commence concept design and budgeting as a time-based charge and then convert to a lump-sum fee when the client gives the go-ahead for the project to proceed. It should also be established that if, for any reason, the client decides not to proceed with the work at any stage after the designer has received instructions, a percentage of the agreed fee will be charged and the designer would also be entitled to reimbursement of all expenses incurred at that stage. Designers should be aware that many clients prefer to see invoices for goods and services supplied by the designer since it gives them more confidence in their work and integrity. This is acceptable practice and should be established at the agreement stage.

When calculating a design fee, designers should consider the time they are likely to spend on each stage of the project as agreed with the client. In addition, they should also consider what the job is actually worth to them and what it is worth on a square-footage basis. As a general rule, budget figures are placed against various elements of the job and then calculated around a set percentage of the total budget cost. This percentage will vary and is likely to be higher for a small project and adjusted downwards for a larger one. In addition to their fee, designers tend to charge expenses for travel, subsistence, out-of-pocket expenses, reproduction of drawings and documents and postage relating specifically to a contract at cost.

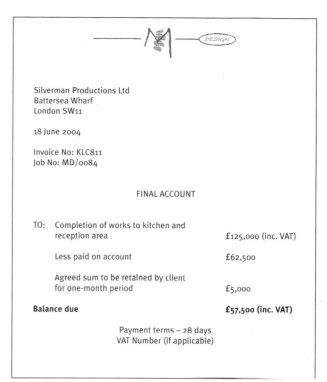

Silverman Productions Ltd
Battersea Wharf
London SW11

18 June 2004

Invoice No: KLC811
Job No: MD/0084

FINAL ACCOUNT

TO:	Completion of works to kitchen and reception area	£125,000 (inc. VAT)
	Less paid on account	£62,500
	Agreed sum to be retained by client for one-month period	£5,000
Balance due		**£57,500 (inc. VAT)**

Payment terms – 28 days
VAT Number (if applicable)

The invoice for the final account would be sent after the official 'handover'. However, an agreed amount over and above this might be retained by the client for a short period in case any post-project problems arise that need the designer's attention.

A summary of the main stages of a project

Stage one

+ Preliminary meeting
+ The client brief
+ The proposal and client's agreement to proposal

Stage two

+ Design survey, measure and analysis
+ Concepts/initial design work
+ Budget costings
+ Preparation of presentation
+ Presentation to client/client's agreement

Stage three

+ Working drawings (which might include lighting and services plans, designs for window treatments and joinery)
+ Specifications/tender documents (against which builders, suppliers, manufacturers and specialists quote for their work)
+ Client estimates
+ Applications to local authorities for consents, as required
+ Appointment of contractors/letters of agreement/contract acceptance

Stage four

+ Job programme
+ Schedule of works
+ Procurement
+ Site supervision, if required
+ Installation of furnishings, if required
+ Completion and handover

Design education
and beyond **VI**

This chapter reviews the personal qualities and attitudes that designers should possess, as well as the skills and knowledge they need to acquire. It discusses the types of education and training available and the ways in which courses are structured. It also offers advice on putting together an appropriate CV (curriculum vitae) and portfolio and finding employment. Finally, there are tips on what to look for and expect from a first job.

Have you got what it takes?

The qualities that you need to succeed as an interior designer are many and varied but there are a few key essentials. You should have a certain level of artistic ability and, in particular, good spatial awareness – a sort of x-ray vision that can bypass the constraints of an existing space and appreciate the design possibilities beyond. (One of the reasons why many people with certain forms of dyslexia are good designers is because of their ability to see three-dimensionally). You should be instinctively looking at the world around you at all times – totally visually aware. There is a view that many people have been attracted into the industry by its apparent glamour and do not have these important instinctive qualities, with the result that they are often make better administrators than designers.

Beyond creativity, a good eye and artistic flair, an open-minded outlook and flexibility of approach will stand you in good stead. The ability to work hard and pay attention to the tiniest detail is of paramount importance as are stamina and a sense of humour. One of the most essential aspects of the work is management of people, whether it is the client, the builders, suppliers or other specialists that make up a project team. The ability to manage in a pleasant yet authoritative way can be the difference between make or break in a project.

To succeed as a designer, you need a certain level of artistic ability and good spatial awareness to appreciate the real possibilities of a space.

While professionals in other industries often require a tunnel vision, interior design work is multifaceted and you need to be good at juggling many different balls. However, since nobody can be good at everything, you should be able to work to your strengths, recognize your own particular weaknesses and make sure that you surround yourself with people who bring to the party any skills that may be lacking to ensure a good, balanced team. Commercial design requires a great deal of complex coordination and usually involves a considerable amount of teamwork. To work in this area, you therefore need to be highly collaborative, practical, flexible and well-versed in the relevant rules, regulations and codes of practice.

Selecting a course of study

Before researching a suitable course of study, a valuable exercise is to think ahead to what your ultimate career goals might be and identify your own strengths, talents and skills and what you particularly enjoy doing. If you are passionate about the more aesthetic side of design – ornament, decoration, the arrangement of furniture, the selection of colours, materials and finishes – it may be that you should concentrate on interior decoration. Although interior designers are of course concerned about the aesthetics of their designs, their focus is on spatial design and finding appropriate creative solutions for the function of an interior.

Once you have identified your career goals, you can start to investigate the methods of study and training required and how to gain entry. Regulation of interior design practice is becoming increasingly widespread and so a suitable formal education is essential. The school leaver is likely to have taken art or art and design at A-level and then, with the advice and encouragement of teachers or career advisors, would usually apply to a foundation course or possibly an access course in order to put together a suitable portfolio to help gain entry to a degree course.

For the career changer, who may not have such a clear sense of direction or the advantage of recent art studies behind them, the route may be different. A fairly typical situation would be someone who had very much enjoyed art and design at school but had been encouraged or persuaded, whether by teachers or parents, to pursue a more traditional career. These people are often extremely successful in their field but, as their role becomes increasingly managerial, feel progressively frustrated that there is no way that they can use or express their creativity. Their interest in interior design often goes right back to the time they had to decide on their A-level choices, but it is frequently a design project of their own that convinces them that interior design is the career change that they want to make.

Some people will decide to pursue the degree route and, in some cases, may gain admission on the grounds of PLE (prior learning experience), but for many career changers who are already graduates this is a step too far. There are some private schools that offer shorter, more intensive, vocational training or diploma courses for mature students wishing to enter the industry, and

Some courses focus primarily on the surface decoration of a space, while others have more of an architectural bias. In an interior such as the restaurant Fifteen in London, there is clearly an emphasis on materials and finishes, but the space also makes a strong statement in terms of its structure.

these can offer an ideal solution. Some may attend local evening classes or short courses to make sure that they are moving in the right direction before making a final decision.

Complementary education or experience outside the areas of art and design might include languages, art history, law and business studies.

When selecting a course of study you should check that the school or college has some sort of recognized accreditation and that the courses it offers are in line with the national requirements and standards of the country concerned. In the US, schools and colleges have the option to apply to FIDER (The Foundation for Interior Design Education Research) for accreditation to show that they meet the standards set by this organization. In the UK, the council for quality control oversees university awards and qualifications and private schools and colleges can opt for an accreditation process through the BAC (British Accreditation Council). Some universities have the power to validate courses and some vocational courses are accredited by City & Guilds, while courses that attract government funding are inspected by OFSTED (Office for Standards in Education).

Courses can vary in length from one to four years and some are delivered via distance learning/home study. To establish whether a programme is suitable for you, it can be helpful to talk to a member of the faculty to find out about the overall approach and ethos of the college and the course aims, objectives and content.

Entry requirements

These vary from college to college and usually include a number of different possible entry routes to encompass other national and international educational qualifications such as the Scottish Certificate of Education, the Irish Leaving Certificate or the International/European Baccalaurcate. Many colleges encourage mature students and so will consider alternative professional or vocational qualifications or experience. Just occasionally, a college will waive the minimum educational qualifications in order to accept an applicant who shows particular promise. In the UK, application is through UCAS route B and potential candidates who satisfy the entry requirements are normally invited for interview to present a portfolio. International candidates may be asked to send a portfolio for review if unable to attend the interview.

In the US, there is much emphasis placed on the content of an applicant's high school programme. In addition to the various units required from this programme, applicants are usually required to make a campus visit

The fundamental aim of all interior design courses is to prepare students for the professional world.

and take either the Scholastic Aptitude Test (SAT) or the American College Test (ACT).

Over and above the entry qualifications, colleges will be looking for evidence of a high potential of creative ability, an appropriate range of skills and the aptitude and motivation to pursue an interior design qualification course successfully.

The college syllabus

The International Federation of Interior Designers stipulates that the curriculum for a design education or training should include the following:

+ *fundamentals of design (philosophy, sociology, aesthetics and a theory of design, visual research, colour, light form, texture);*
+ *basic knowledge of materials (wood, metal, plastic, fabric and so forth);*
+ *visual communication (objective and interpretative drawing, freehand perspective drawing, use of colour media, photography and model-making);*
+ *people in their environment (human ergonometric and anthropometric studies and design evaluation, history of art and architecture, interiors and furniture);*
+ *creative work by the project method (a minimum of four major projects);*
+ *information input and briefing, design analysis, design exploration, design solutions submitted in a visual form;*
+ *interpretation of the project schemes and technical studies related to the built environment (working drawings, building technology, understanding of structure and services);*
+ *costing and estimating, detailing and specifying materials, furniture and fittings;*
+ *professional practice (verbal communication techniques, office organization and practice, legislation affecting the designer, visiting projects that are in the course of being made or built).*

Just occasionally, a college will waive the minimum educational qualifications in order to accept an applicant who demonstrates particular promise.

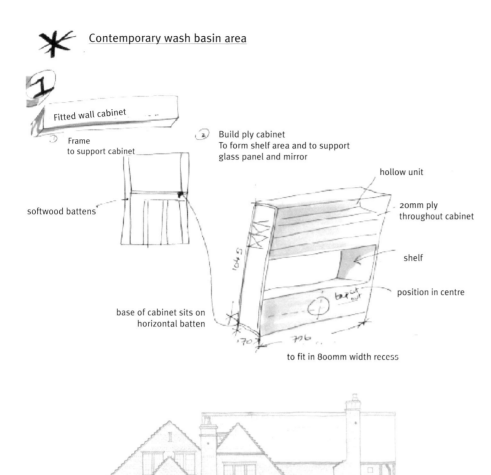

Contemporary wash basin area

Fitted wall cabinet

Frame
to support cabinet

Build ply cabinet
To form shelf area and to support
glass panel and mirror

softwood battens

hollow unit

20mm ply
throughout cabinet

shelf

position in centre

base of cabinet sits on
horizontal batten

to fit in 800mm width recess

Left Sketching and attention to detail are much encouraged on a design course.

Below Recording architectural detail is a good way to learn how buildings are constructed.

While curricula may vary in content and approach, the basic strategy is the same, which is to prepare students for the professional world by allowing their interests and ambitions to mature through a combination of theoretical and technical aspects. Interior design students are encouraged to develop a critical understanding of the creation and habitation of space and to allow their practical and intellectual development to expand in tandem with their personal expression and creativity.

Design studies do not represent an easy option and are rigorous and demanding, although ultimately exceptionally rewarding. Architectural and design history and contextual studies are regarded as key elements in an interior design course as they allow students to understand interior design as a spatial dimension of culture and social interaction. Initially, considerable time is spent on the development of the fundamental skills: surveying and drawing techniques; scale and proportion; two- and three-dimensional exercises; and visualization with a focus on form, scale, colour and light. In many programmes, life drawing is seen as the primary source of design, and students are encouraged to make constant use of their sketchbooks, observing and recording to build up a rich source of ideas and inspiration.

Creative expression in project work is fostered, but emphasis is placed on technical viability and sensitivity to those using the space. A great emphasis in interior design courses is now placed on the design studio and teaching methodology, and the project work undertaken in the studio is arguably the most important part of a course. This is because the brief

Life drawing helps students to understand how much space is needed for people to lie, stand and sit.

provided will not only have clear objectives and assessment criteria but will also be a simulation of the sort of work the student can expect to become involved in after graduation and will ultimately provide a basis for the portfolio.

As a course progresses, the focus tends to be on developing skills in problem analysis, design methodology and design decision-making. Students will also start to develop a personal design vision. With exposure to so many different styles and stimuli, tastes inevitably develop and change throughout a designer's life. It will be important for students to be able to absorb and benefit from the different stylistic influences to which they are exposed, while starting to find the courage and vision to develop their own style and personal expression.

Practical studies cover building construction, detailing and creative computing, while design specialisms include product, furniture, lighting, retail and exhibition design, perhaps with additional project options in film and television design, hospitality and leisure. Analysis and research form an important part of project work. Students are encouraged to explore the use of materials in order to become competent and confident in their application. Key personal skills, such as communication and teamwork, are included as part of the creative development process and emphasis is placed on self-direction and time-management.

Towards the end of a course, interior design practice management, information technology, studies in aesthetics, and design and creative enterprise (which might include areas such as marketing and market research or design branding) are often introduced. In the final year, students often

Field trips to museums, exhibitions, galleries, showrooms and design practices form part of the curriculum of most interior design courses and are a valuable and stimulating part of a student's studies.

undertake a dissertation in addition to their final project which in some colleges may be self-initiated. Project work tends to increase in size and scale as the course progresses, and so public services and large-scale urban interiors might be included in the latter part of a course.

The demands of these courses and the absorbing nature of design work can be exhausting, and it is important for students to pace themselves and make sure that they have a reasonable amount of sleep and good nutrition. Creativity requires high levels of energy.

In the latter part of a course, advice is given on career planning and development and portfolio presentation. There are often opportunities to take part in national student competitions and to enter internships or placements that can be a particularly valuable support to the more theoretical studies. Field trips to trade fairs, exhibitions, museums, galleries and design practices are also included.

The graduate show

The culmination of an interior design course is always the graduate show that provides a forum for prospective employers. To take advantage of this valuable opportunity, students will work with tutors to put together a display of work that shows off their skills, originality and potential and, ideally, is tailored towards the sort of work they would like to do in the future. Consistent graphics and well-produced business cards play an important part in the overall impression of a stand. Students are usually expected to attend the show throughout its duration in order to answer queries and promote their work and that of their fellow students. After the show, they can follow up any promising leads, reorganize their portfolio and start hunting for a job.

Assessment

Throughout a course, students are given a clear idea of assessment requirements and criteria and are provided with in-depth feedback to help them identify strengths and weaknesses and areas for improvement. Methods of assessment might include practical projects, oral presentations, practical assignments and peer assessment, and students would be encouraged to consider and evaluate their own performance. Criticism should never be regarded as personal and it is important for students to remain positive and open-minded and to understand that they cannot simply impose their designs on a client.

Design courses are usually delivered through a combination of structured teaching and independent study, with students becoming increasingly responsible for managing their own learning as a course progresses. Formal lectures are often supplemented by seminars allowing discussion between students and teaching staff.

Degrees are usually awarded at different levels: first-class honours, upper second, second, and third class, but some colleges simply award a pass. (Other qualifications such as certificates and diplomas have distinction, merit

Opposite The end-of-year show represents the culmination of all the students' hard graft. Work is displayed with a view to catching the eye of a prospective employer and students are encouraged to show a variety of presentation methods and to display different facets of their work.

Below Constructive feedback on a student's project work forms an important part of any interior design course.

and pass classifications). Usually, there are marks for written work, such as a thesis, computed into the total; the balance and percentage given to contextual studies will vary in different establishments.

In the unlikely event of a failure, a college is required to indicate what the problems were and may suggest that a project or examination is done again. If students are unhappy with their marks at any point during their course of study they should arrange to see their tutors and discuss the problem. Teaching staff are always keen to see their students do well; all colleges have appeal systems and many have social-welfare programmes in place to help those in difficulties.

The future of design education

The role of design education is to provide students with the fundamental knowledge and skills required in the industry. Technological skills will form an increasingly crucial part of this education without diminishing the importance of creative skills such as drawing and three-dimensional visualization. Course work will become thoroughly integrated so that, for example, Computer-Aided Design (CAD) will be a subsidiary class taken by students alongside other design classes. Specialist software packages are already available which, combined with Internet research, can help students build up trade reference libraries, and these provide a particularly valuable resource for environmentally friendly materials and information about sustainable design. Courses will need to take account of the rapid development of technology in the world at large and the effects that advanced household technology have on people's lifestyles. The provision of interior design education is evolving in itself, with computers being used for Powerpoint Lectures and online courses.

From a global point of view, ecology, energy consumption and an ageing society will be some of the main themes at the heart of design in the future. Design education will need to address issues such as the specification of fewer toxic materials and the reduction of energy consumption and carbon dioxide discharge in order to protect the environment. Ageing society is another important issue that should be addressed in the courses of the future. In Japan, and many other countries, a quarter of the population will be over 65 years old in 2025 and there will be a vital need for designers to create sustainable and affordable homes suitable for this older population. The increasing emphasis on the holistic side of design will also need to be reflected in interior design education.

It is widely believed that design education needs to become more structured and technical and that the professional practice content of degree courses should give them parity with architectural degrees. Course titles would reflect their particular focus and more flexible education such as part-time degrees could be introduced as further encouragement of mature students to study and qualify.

Design education is also likely to broaden in scope to include relevant areas of study such as business, law and finance and to focus more on verbal

There is an increasing emphasis on environmental considerations in design education. The greenhouse construction of this house at Lyon-St-Just, France (Jourdan and Perraudin), combined with canvas, insulation and planting, is designed to create an eco-friendly environment.

and written communication skills. One fundamental area of design that deserves fresh attention is creativity and it is vital that design education works to promote the highest levels of creative problem-solving so that innovation is revered alongside technical ability.

There is further diversification among degree courses to provide more dedicated interior design degrees and MA and Phd courses in interior design are now available in many parts of the world. These higher areas of study will become more desirable with the growing need for research and development in interior design projects. The value of continuous lifelong learning for the interior designer is now fully recognized in line with many other professions.

The importance of qualifications

It is increasingly acknowledged internationally that it is not acceptable for people to call themselves an interior designer without the proper qualifications. These qualifications ensure that a designer is capable of delivering a particular level of knowledge and service and require constant review so that the public is well-protected, particularly with regard to health, safety and welfare issues.

Many countries operate a licensing system for interior designers wishing to set up their own practice. To obtain this licence, certain criteria must be met. In the US, eighteen states already require a licence to practise and in due course mandatory nationwide licensure may be brought in. Candidates wishing to sit the NCIDQ (National Council for Interior Design Qualification) professional interior design examination in the US need a minimum of two years of interior design education plus four years of work experience in interior design to be eligible (the longer the design education undertaken the shorter the work experience element becomes). The educational requirements are evaluated as follows:

> *Five years*
> At least 150 semester credits (of which 90 or more are related to interior design), 225 quarter credits (of which 135 or more are related to interior design)
> *Four years*
> At least 120 semester credits (of which 60 or more are related to interior design), 180 quarter credits (of which 90 or more are related to interior design)
> *Three years*
> At least 60 semester credits or 90 quarter credits of course work related to interior design)
> *Two years*
> At least 40 semester credits or 60 quarter credits of course work related to interior design

For graduates of accredited interior design courses, NCIDQ operates a work-experience programme to provide a transition between formal education and professional practice. This involves 3,520 hours of recorded work experience in a practice supported and guided by a supervisor and a mentor. Unfortunately, there is no international industry standard but professional associations within the industry also play an important role in raising standards of practice, increasing respect for the professional designer and helping to protect the general public from unqualified and unprofessional operators.

Agreed minimal standards have not yet been established in the UK and so to some extent it remains an unprotected profession. In Russia, where interior design and decoration have only really developed as a profession in the last ten years, a licensing system has been introduced and the need for a solid design education is recognized. After many years of standard 'state allocated' apartments, today there is a far greater choice of homes offered by the Russian building market. This varies from country or town houses, cottages or penthouses to economic one- or two-bedroom apartments or studios. Many practising Russian designers are often highly educated with degrees in history of art, languages, economics, psychology and law, all of which can be very useful when working on interior design projects. However, focused training that provides a systematic approach to what a designer must accomplish is also required.

With licensing aspects coming into play in the near future in the US, there will probably be much less room for entering the profession without the proper education, experience and testing. However, the licensing of architects has led to a clear division of the art into the craft of building and actual architecture. This has meant that the general consumer tends to buy buildings from a developer, while architecture is seen as a serious commodity purchased by an affluent few. There is therefore the risk that generalized licensing of interior designers might lead to a similar separation between the actual art and its function, and so the industry will need to ensure that a careful balance is preserved in order that interior design does not become totally elitist.

Finding employment

Interior design is a relatively new profession and there is not really a tried-and-tested entry route. It is important, therefore, to build up contacts and to network during your design education or training at every possible opportunity. Although some companies do recruit from university graduates,

It has been suggested that architecture has become too elitist in recent years and so it is encouraging to see developers showing design sensitivity and awareness of the importance of community.

Finding employment 157

A CV checklist

Personal details (name, address, phone/fax/email)

Short mission statement, if required, detailing job expectations and perceived personal qualities

Education/training (to include short description of courses and any awards received)

Employment history

Additional relevant skills (e.g. computer literacy, languages, driving licence, etc.)

Interests and activities

AMY THOMAS

12 Tulip Avenue, Green Lane, London, SW2 04P
Tel: 0201 862572 **Mobile:** 01864 792364 **email:** amy.thomas@home.co.uk

I am a hard-working and focused graduate designer looking for a position that will give me good experience across the board and consolidate my training. My strengths include generating concepts, sourcing materials and finishes, and design realization.

Education & qualifications

2000–2003 KLC School of Design
Honours Diploma in Interior Design & Decoration
Course elements include: design theory, planning; technical drawing; rendering; lighting; history of style; CAD (Vector Works)

1996–1997 Weston University
Masters in Personnel Management
CIPD Professional Qualification (Grad Membership)

1991–1995 Aberystwyth University
BA (Hons) Economics 2:1

1984–1991 St. James's Convent
'A' Levels: English, Art, Maths with Statistics
11 GCSE passes all at grade A

Career history & work experience

April 2003 Todhunter Earl, London
Internship

Dec 1999–Oct 2002 HSBC, London
Global Markets HR Advisor
• HR Advisor for the Global Markets Graduate Classes
• Management of the Global Placement Office
• Management of London-based Global Markets Organizational/Management Development Initiatives including:
Executive Coaching; Performance Management On-Line; Senior Leadership Programmes; Employment Law Training

Sept 1997–Oct 1999 Citi Bank, London
Training & Development Officer
• Management of the London Graduate Development & Summer Intern Programmes to Corporate Finance,
Global Markets & IT

Summer 1997 Deloitte & Touche, London
Summer Internship

June 1995–Sept 1996 Progrent Ltd, Hertfordshire
Sales Representative

June 199 –Sept 1993 Trendall Systems Intl. Hampshire
Industrial Placement Student

Additional information

Winner of the Student Competition 2003 to design an exhibition stand
Highly proficient in a wide range of software packages, including MS Word, Excel, PowerPoint
Full clean driving licence
Hobbies including tennis, scuba diving, watercolour painting, DIY, travel, gardening

References available on request

you will need to carry out your own research on suitable companies or practices in which to work.

The aim of networking is to help you make links with individuals and organizations within the industry that could help you identify and explore opportunities and thus increase your employability. The skill of effective networking is not to pester but to be a good communicator. Of course, if you notice that a company has just gained a contract for a project, it may be worth contacting it to see if extra help is needed.

Networking can be done through personal contacts such as friends, ex-colleagues and family members, as well as college tutors who are experienced professionals with their own network of contacts. It can also be useful to contact relevant organizations and associations and to be proactive in terms of taking work-experience placements or additional short training courses. Make the most of any contacts you establish by keeping records of a person's details, when the contact was made and when follow-up action would be needed, and always have your CV and business card ready.

There are a myriad opportunities available for interior designers, both currently and in the future. As a design graduate, you will need to consider what will suit you best in terms of interest, consolidation of your education or training, or in terms of laying the foundation for any chosen career progression. You will need to decide whether to concentrate on residential or commercial work, whether you would ideally prefer a small company or a large one, whether you would like to be in a multi-disciplinary practice (perhaps an architectural one within which there is an interior design department), work for a furniture or home furnishings store or specialize in a particular area of design such as retail, exhibition, medical or kitchen and bathroom. Many people also consider making the transition to sales or representation during their career or education. As the profession becomes better established and more valued by society generally, the career possibilities increase. For example, there may be firms that practise other design disciplines in addition to interior design and architecture and, in the US particularly, this might include engineering or urban design with projects in the commercial, residential, retail, hospitality, medical, government and education sectors.

Employment prospects for interior designers are particularly good in the US and are rapidly improving in Europe. According to a report from the US Department of Labor's Bureau of Labor Statistics, the news is positive:

Overall, the employment of designers is expected to grow faster than the average through the year 2010. In addition to those that result from employment growth, job openings will arise from the need to replace designers who leave the field. Rising demand for professional design of private homes, offices, restaurants and other retail establishments and institutions that care for the rapidly growing elderly population should spur employment growth of interior designers.

Applying for jobs

A creative, imaginative and committed approach to job searching is the key to success. A good portfolio is usually needed in order to approach potential employers. Some job seekers set up websites featuring their CV and portfolio, although it is important to check for excessive download times of any graphic elements in the site, as these can work against you.

It will obviously be essential to keep up to date with developments in the design industry, both during and after your design education. When you are ready to start job-hunting the first thing to do is to identify the opportunities available to you and to try and decide on the direction you want to take. In this way you can make your research and networking as specific as possible.

Understandably, companies prefer to recruit from a known source whether it is a college or university they have recruited from before or a contact made through someone already in their employ. For that reason, it makes sense to visit friends already working in a practice, perhaps meeting with them and their colleagues after work so that if a vacancy does come up, you are not unknown to them. In the same way, work experience and internships can provide not only valuable and confidence-boosting experience but also sometimes a route into employment.

There are agencies that specialize in placing people in the interior design industry and a few publications carry advertisements for recruitment, but very often it will be up to the individual to research suitable companies to apply to. It is likely that any company, practice or individual to which you are applying will be regularly inundated with CVs and applications and you will need to think of ways to make yours stand out. Quality of presentation and originality of content are advantageous but avoid anything too flamboyant or in poor taste. You will also need to show that you have done research on the company since if you fail to make reference to the type of work undertaken, your application is unlikely to get past the first hurdle.

There are different schools of thought on the content of CVs but as a general rule it is best to keep them concise. Rather than laboriously listing everything you have studied or every element of any previous experience, it is best to limit yourself to points that are totally relevant to the work you might undertake for the company concerned. Many employers, however, appreciate a relatively full CV set out in chronological order with education listed before the actual work experience. Quite often, CVs will go straight to the human resources department in a company and only a select few will actually reach the desk of the ultimate decision-maker.

Whatever the progress of a CV, first impressions are all-important. Give careful consideration to the typeface, type of paper and colours that you use. You could opt for a classic CV executed to perfection or one in a more contemporary style, perhaps accompanied by examples of your work.

The letter accompanying your CV requires an equal amount of thought. Although it can afford to be a little less formal than the CV itself, it is likely to be carefully scrutinized and you need to express yourself effectively. It is here that you can demonstrate that you have researched the company, or mention that you admire the work of the designer you are approaching. You should also state what you believe you have to offer, as well as what you are looking for.

The portfolio

Interior design is, above all, a visual subject and although a qualification is undoubtedly a key priority, it will be the quality of your portfolio that will swing the final decision. It is therefore really worth spending the time to think through how you are going to display your work to the best effect. At the end of your course, your work is likely to be in chronological order but at the job-seeking stage there are advantages to dismantling the work and sorting it into piles, with the best at the front. A portfolio should not look too full or too empty. Edit out any project work that does not show your strengths; from the work remaining, assemble the projects to show not only your completed design solutions but also your research and the design development.

Order the work so that you start with something strong and finish with a good conversation piece. Consider including a colour photocopy of an effective visual and have a business card to hand so that you can leave both items with the interviewer. Try to create a cohesive look in the portfolio. Plastic sleeves often come with a black backing paper which can provide a good background for artwork, but neutrals can be an effective alternative. Many practices still put a great deal of emphasis on technical drawing and detail drawings and an interviewer is likely to be looking for precision, accuracy and a stylish technique. It is also important to ensure that each project is clearly defined and titled. Prospective employers are likely to appreciate the chance to see some printed examples of CAD work in the portfolio. You might like to make colour copies of your entire portfolio since colour copies can look better than the originals, although there is a slight risk that the interviewer will question whether the work is authentic. Large drawings often look better when reduced and sketches will look more professional if presented at the same size.

As you find out more about the companies that you are going to attend for interview you may find that you have to adapt your portfolio to suit their particular specializations. Always check your portfolio through before an interview to make sure that it is clear, cohesive and impressive.

Work placements and internships

These can provide a very valuable way of easing yourself into the industry and gaining experience that will enhance the CV. They also provide a useful way to try out different career paths and make valuable contacts for future networking. The work may be fairly menial to begin with but some practices will give more responsibility as you progress. It really pays to look the part, work hard and keep good time. Many colleges are very proactive about this

Putting your portfolio together

The quality of your portfolio will play a crucial role in the job-seeking process. Make sure the work you choose reflects your strengths and aim for clarity and cohesion. It is a good idea to include material from each stage of the design process, as shown here, but you may need to adapt the contents to suit the particular specializations and interests of a prospective employer.

The Spencer Club Refurbishment The weekend Business Lounge Jane Ranson 2004

Concept board.

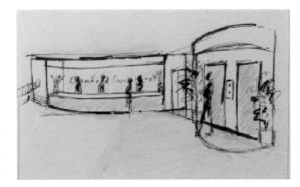

Concept sketch.

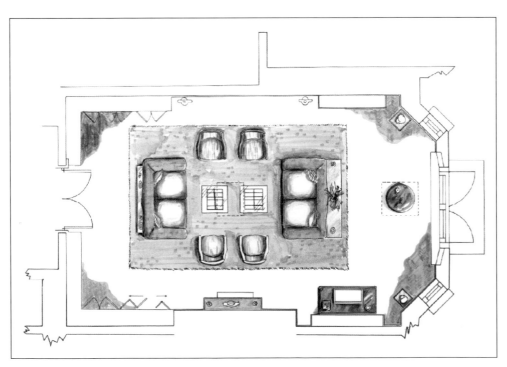

Plan.

Perspective drawing.

Axonometric.

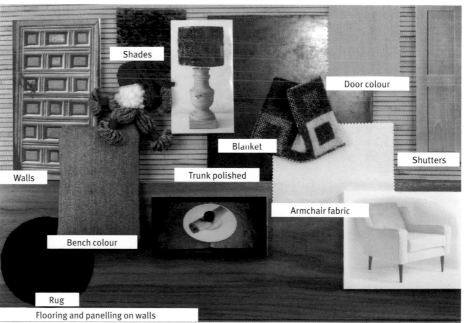

Shades

Door colour

Blanket

Shutters

Walls

Trunk polished

Armchair fabric

Bench colour

Rug

Flooring and panelling on walls

Sample board.

and will help with placements in the breaks between terms or run sandwich courses of which an internship is an integral part. The student is often asked to write an evaluation report and so it is advisable to keep a work diary and ask colleagues for any information that could be included. Employers may also be asked to fill in a form or give verbal feedback. In some instances, these work-experience sessions or internships work so well for both sides involved that it may lead to permanent employment for the student concerned.

The interview

Research your potential employers so that you can demonstrate that you know their work and can speak knowledgeably about their design style. Time your arrival well. Be early, but not too early, and certainly never be late. Ensure you locate the office beforehand, if necessary, so that you arrive feeling as calm and composed as possible. It is essential to be enthusiastic about the job you are applying for, since if you give the impression that you might be perfectly happy doing something else you are highly unlikely to get the job. Appearances are important, too. In the context of a design practice this does not necessarily mean having to appear in a traditional suit but for an interview, jeans and trainers are not acceptable. You should look immaculate and wear something that indicates your sense of style, as an interviewer is likely to take the view that if you care about your appearance then you are likely to care about your work and the all-important small details. Many of the best designers are fastidious about personal appearance.

Manner is equally important, and you need to strike the right balance. You need to show confidence without appearing arrogant, but to demonstrate enough strength of character to convince the interviewer that you are capable of handling difficult clients, since this may be necessary even in a junior position. Have two or three well-planned questions written in a neat and stylish notebook (to demonstrate your organizational skills), but bear in mind that you are not the one conducting the interview and avoid dominating the conversation.

Your first job

A valuable way to approach your first job is to regard it as the second part of your design training or education. However good a design education you may have had, it is not possible to simulate the difficult client or the amount of time required to carry out the more mundane administrative parts of the work. Although you will never stop learning throughout your career, your first job should consolidate everything you have learnt on your course.

For people entering the industry it can be a very good move to join one of the professional associations and to start to contribute to that association and the industry as a whole. It is important not to be intimidated by those who have more experience than you in the industry and it is always worthwhile establishing good relationships with other designers.

Careers **VII**

This final chapter presents the different career options open to the trained interior designer and suggests opportunities for specialization and personal development. It stresses the need for the constant updating of design skills and knowledge, as well as the importance of exchanging information between professionals nationally and internationally. In conclusion, it reflects on possible future developments in the industry.

Residential design

While interior design breaks down into two main categories – commercial and residential – there is a huge variety of work within and beyond these areas.

Residential work can include the specialist areas of colour consultancy, children's rooms, kitchens and bathrooms, furniture design and, increasingly, design for the disabled. Estate agents sometimes employ in-house designers to provide a space-planning and design service for purchasers and to advise on interiors for rental.

Commercial design

Commercial design is the most popular and competitive area of specialization and in the US, up to 80 percent of design graduates are currently entering the commercial sector.

The types of jobs available to designers will always be dependent on the particular needs of a country's population. One notable trend in recent years has come about as a result of increasingly ageing populations, which is driving the building and design industries more towards leisure provision, healthcare and sheltered housing.

Retail

Interior design for retail outlets and wholesale showrooms is a popular specialist area, but within these specializations there are also opportunities for visual merchandising, lighting design and related careers such as sales management and buying. Retail design offers considerable scope for the designer and encompasses boutiques, department stores, factory-outlet stores, discount retailing, shopping centres and any service business that deals directly with its customers. Retail design is totally commercial, a strategic tool geared to creating sales on a per-square-foot basis. The contemporary approach is all about strategic brand development and creating a customer 'experience' through an environment that reflects the aspirations of the general public. The retail designer understands that a customer is buying into complex, intangible elements as much as purchasing specific goods or services.

Exhibitions

Exhibition design can include trade, temporary or museum exhibitions. It can be very stimulating work since it often involves an academic element and

Retail design has become an exciting and multifaceted area of specialization for the interior designer.

Commercial design **167**

Curved counters and lighting grids help to guide customers around this sportswear shop in Los Angeles and also provide the basis for eye-catching displays.

A design for an exhibition stand at the annual trade fair Decorex in London, 2003. The brief was to design a striking show-stand for a company specializing in limestone products. It was also important to allow ample space for visitors to talk to representatives of the company within the stand itself.

can require a designer to create a total experience for visitors. There may be considerable historical research involved and a wide range of planning that encompasses chronological ordering of displays, traffic flow, lighting and even sound effects.

Hospitality and entertainment

Another much sought-after area of design work is hospitality and entertainment, which includes hotels, restaurants, clubs, bars, cafés, conference centres, cruise ships, casinos, cinemas, theatres, spas and gymnasiums, and even amusement parks. For this sort of work, it is important for the designer to gain an understanding of every aspect of the client's business, from the operational image and functional requirements through to the budget and financial constraints. These will be clients who regard the design work as an investment, and the designer will need to work not only to budget but to relate designs to the clients' ideas while ensuring the long-term quality and wear of the design, materials and finishes. Within the categories of hospitality and entertainment design, some practices will specialize further, focusing exclusively on yacht design, for example, or hotels and restaurants.

Good hospitality design requires an understanding of commerce and
marketing in addition to the obvious design skills.

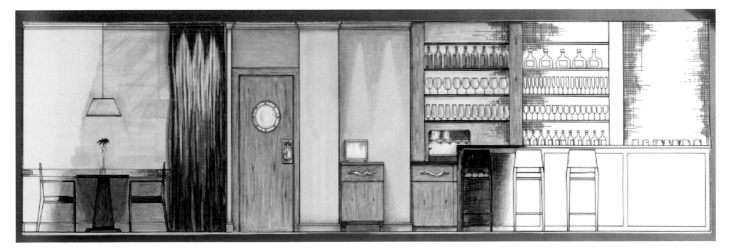

Hospitality design has become one of the most sought-after areas of design in
recent years with the increase of restaurants and hotels of all types, including
the much-coveted boutique hotel.

Hospitality and entertainment design

Many holiday-makers and travellers select hotels as much for their design as for their facilities and amenities. The sleek lines of the lobby in the HI Hotel in Nice, for example, would appeal to those who appreciate clean, modern lines and finishes.

Entertainment centres such as theatres, cinemas and casinos represent a dynamic area of interior design specialization.

One of the most important elements in hospitality design is lighting, which can be used to create mood and style as well as to define specific spaces.

Some of the most cutting-edge and creative interior design work is to be found in bars and restaurants where the concept and branding are taken right through to the menus and table settings.

In this hospital in Indiana by architect Robert Stern, a palette of warm, restful colours has been employed to create an atmosphere of calm.

Medical and educational

Medically orientated work such as designing hospitals, clinics, hospices, rest homes, sheltered housing and consulting rooms offers another area of specialization. Healthcare design is expanding to meet the demand for alternative and complementary forms of treatment, including provisions for care in the home and workplace. Budget and practical considerations are likely to be of paramount importance here, but the healthcare designer will also be concerned with convenience, accessibility, confidentiality and the creation of a suitably holistic environment. Designing interiors for educational establishments, including nurseries, schools, colleges and universities, is another career option within the public sphere.

Offices

As working patterns become more flexible, traditional office design has opened up, allowing the designer much greater scope than ever before. Whether working on individual, interactive or shared workspaces, the designer will need to take the time to learn about and understand every aspect of the business, its objectives and the project targets in relation to current activities and future growth. This might be done through interviews with staff involved, surveys, questionnaires or simple observation.

In some interior design practices, the majority of design work is done on computer. For graduates who particularly enjoy computer work, there are opportunities to work as CAD operators or as virtual reality designers.

This multifunctional office area could be used for presentations, meetings or business entertaining.

Changing working habits provide the designer with new challenges: shared workspaces for shift workers; hot-desking or unassigned workplaces; home offices for telecommuters; satellite offices that allow people to work closer to home; and the provision of the virtual office, set up so that busy executives can work in a hotel room or while travelling. Computer-aided design is a particularly valuable tool that helps the designer establish space requirements and develop suitable layouts. This type of design carries great responsibility since the designer must create a safe and healthy environment while meeting the functional, practical and aesthetic needs of clients within a given budget and with a view to increasing productivity and quality of life.

Other areas of specialization

Some large companies offer employment in their in-house design departments, planning and designing for various company needs, and there is also interesting work to be found with product manufacturers and suppliers of furniture, fabric and lighting on the design, marketing or promotional sides or as industry representatives. Graduate designers may also find employment as CAD operators, lighting or virtual-reality designers. There are also opportunities internationally with design consultancies, whether they specialize in interior design, or architectural or multi-disciplinary work. In addition, there are a variety of para-design occupations in industries such as film, fashion, theatre, public relations, marketing and journalism as well as opportunities in education (this usually requires an additional qualifying year) or research for the design profession.

Event design for weddings, parties and other social events is a growth area, as is visualization, which might include illustration work for clients or point-of-sale and window displays in areas of visual merchandising. There are opportunities to create inspirational interiors within the media and advertising industries or to design show houses, apartments and rental properties, which is a small but rewarding specialist area.

Sometimes a designer will be asked to design details such as menus, table settings or even staff uniforms.

In designing show houses, a designer needs to develop a complete understanding of the target market and convey the type of lifestyle that will suit the potential customer. Here, the look is sleek and contemporary and would most obviously appeal to young, urban professionals.

The future of the industry

Interior design has, to an extent, lived under the shadow of architecture for many years. Clearer distinctions are now beginning to emerge between these two related professions that, once established, should help to define interior design as a well-respected profession with ethics, values, vision and purpose. The profession as a whole will then be in a better position to address important questions about design ideology, lifestyle, safety, comfort and human behaviour, and to encourage the sensory and perceptual aspects of interior design in addition to function and ergonomics.

The future for the interior design industry looks promising. Many nations are now fully design-conscious and this is a situation that can only continue. As consumers increasingly recognize the value of good design in relation to health, safety and welfare issues and, in particular, to quality of life, the industry will continue to thrive. More and more, businesses will appreciate the power of high-quality interior design, whether as a result of increased sales in an ultra-sharp retail space or improved efficiency in an ergonomically designed work environment.

Global growth

Continuing globalization will require a designer to address issues of both global identity and local or regional autonomy with knowledge and sensitivity. Manufacturers will compete on a global basis with highly competitive manufacturing from Asia. China will be a major growth area for interior design, and in Japan, exciting contemporary design will continue to develop. Design innovation will continue largely from Europe and the US, as well as from Australia where interior design is a growing industry, both domestically and commercially.

Today's economies which are embracing commercial, leisure, educational and exhibition design as new phenomena are focused on the Pacific Rim and, to a lesser extent, the Middle East. Practices based in the US and Europe are likely to continue to develop their client portfolios in these parts of the world, although this may diminish as countries such as China, Hong Kong and other economies develop their own design schools.

Interior design will continue to be a growth industry in many European countries where it is a relatively new profession: for example, in countries like Portugal where the profession has developed mainly in the last ten years and business is increasing as the confidence of the public grows. In countries such as Russia, the future of the interior design profession will depend to some extent on whether the economic growth and improved quality of life are maintained. Currently, the rights of designers in Russia who take on private work on a part-time or freelance basis are not always protected, and so many designers prefer to have permanent employment with major design or architectural firms. In Japan, experts believe that although there is great potential for the interior design market to grow substantially, only a few interior designers have the status of architects, who tend to dominate the industry, and so it will be essential to foster high standards among the interior professions for growth to occur successfully.

Blurring of boundaries

Individual customization will drive the creation of new types of amenities, which will become more complex and comprehensive. The blurring of distinct functions will continue to change architecture typologies: for

Amenity functions are becoming increasingly blurred in interior design, as witnessed by this music store-cum-café. The challenge for the designer is to create layouts that encourage customers to move comfortably around the space and to take advantage of the different amenities on offer.

example, shops that double as cafés; boutiques combined with libraries; or spa-like living spaces for the elderly.

There will be an increasing cross-over between the different disciplines and, in some quarters, the distinction between different types of design, namely residential and commercial, will continue to break down, with the emphasis shifting to client-centred design. Signature designers will cross global boundaries and will be recognized celebrities throughout the world, while the majority of design will continue to be carried out on a local and regional basis. Collaboration between designers and design firms will also traverse global boundaries in order to accommodate and service the 'global client'.

Design styles will, of course, continue to change. To a large extent, traditional styles will be replaced by interiors that, while simpler in appearance, will be more complicated in execution. Minimalism, in the form of simplified, pared-down interiors, is likely to remain and there will be more demand for an individual, almost *haute couture* approach to interior design, particularly in urban areas. Demand for classic, comfortable interiors that balance practicality with timeless elegance is, however, almost certain to continue.

Developments in professional practice

Technology will continue to advance and influence how work and services are performed in the form of three-dimensional visualizations, Internet product information and product research. It will also progress from being a 'bolt-on' to becoming a thoroughly integrated part of interior design, as clients demand the latest in home entertainment and services control. This, in turn, will trigger new approaches in systems design. Good, clean lines with beautiful natural materials will become commonplace, with antiques and artworks being made to stand out as spectacular features in an otherwise pure environment. The designer will need to stay up to date with these trends and work with specialist suppliers and craftsmen to deliver a happy marriage of form and function.

A more negative development will be the growth of litigation in the area of professional practice. It will become increasingly vital for designers to carry appropriate insurances as protection. One of the benefits a professional association can provide is advice and support in the event of a client-designer relationship breaking down and, if necessary, arbitration services. The professional associations have much to offer the designers of the future in the way of support services, ongoing education and training, and the invaluable opportunity for networking at national and international levels.

Terminology in the industry

Terminology in the interior design industry has become somewhat confused, and it would be helpful for the profession as a whole to define itself in ways that are consistent and recognizable internationally.

Planning a career in interior design

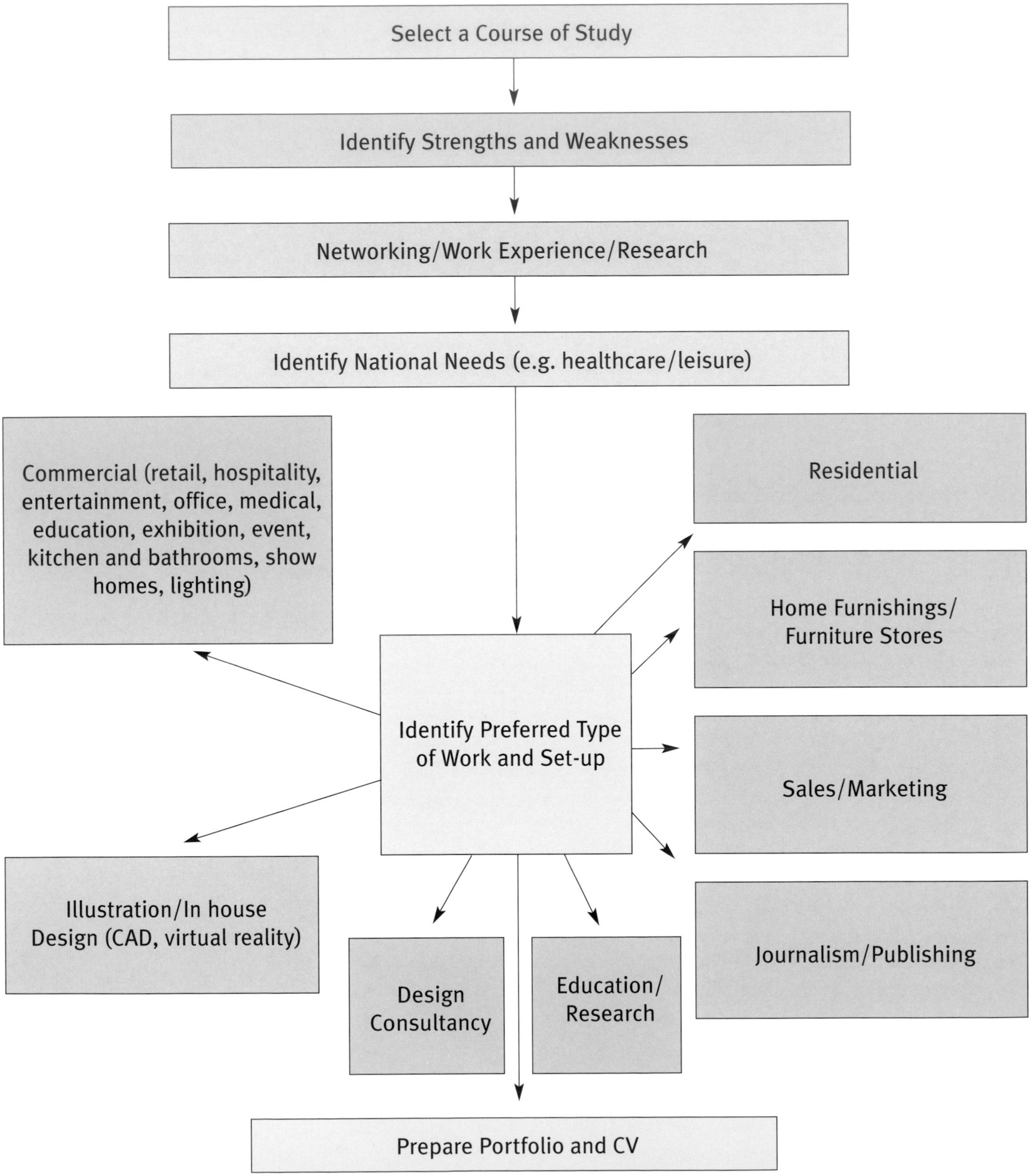

Select a Course of Study

↓

Identify Strengths and Weaknesses

↓

Networking/Work Experience/Research

↓

Identify National Needs (e.g. healthcare/leisure)

↓

Identify Preferred Type of Work and Set-up

Commercial (retail, hospitality, entertainment, office, medical, education, exhibition, event, kitchen and bathrooms, show homes, lighting)

Residential

Home Furnishings/ Furniture Stores

Sales/Marketing

Journalism/Publishing

Illustration/In house Design (CAD, virtual reality)

Design Consultancy

Education/ Research

Prepare Portfolio and CV

Despite the fact that the industry is achieving recognition throughout the world as a discrete profession and not just a subset of architecture, a professional in the industry in parts of the US and Europe is often referred to as an interior architect. In the UK, however, this is not currently possible since the Royal Institute of British Architects has the title 'architect' protected by its charter. The only difference between an interior designer and an interior architect would seem to be that the latter might take on slightly larger projects.

In Japan, there are 36,000 qualified interior coordinators, 3,600 lifestyle planners and 1,800 interior planners, all of whom work mainly as interior decorators in the residential market since architects have a much higher status and tend to control design projects.

The term 'interior decorator' is usually applied to someone who is mainly concerned with surface decoration, style and atmosphere, whose work includes the soft furnishings and interior appointments but not the spatial modifications. An interior designer is responsible for these elements, too, but also works on spatial reconfiguration, changing or modifying actual room sizes (always, it must be stressed, in consultation with a structural engineer) and dealing with lighting. Both interior designers and decorators often work in tandem with architects. With an increasingly design-literate and visually aware public, interior designers will need to distinguish themselves as serious professionals who provide substantial expertise unavailable from any other professional, especially architects and interior decorators.

Two different types of interior designers are likely to evolve: the generalist and the specialist. This is already happening in the US. The specialists will require a depth of creative, technical and practical knowledge currently often lacking.

Technology has become an integral part of the design process. Here, a CAD-generated visual brings to life a design for a club-room bar.

The layout of the twenty-first-century home needs to be flexible. In this guest room, which doubles as a home office, discreet cupboards have been designed to hide away all the technology when it is not in use.

A holistic approach

As we move further into the twenty-first century, the interior designer will need to be flexible and adapt to ever-changing styles and trends. An area of concerted growth will be the quantifiable attributes of emotional, sensory and comfort-generating environments as we search for ecologically safe and natural materials and turn increasingly to nature in a troubled and highly industrialized world. There will be greater emphasis on specifying environmentally friendly materials, with lower operating costs and energy efficiency making 'green' products increasingly attractive to designers and clients alike. A home will be valued more in terms of its atmosphere than as a representation of material wealth. Services in the behavioural analysis of an area will also enter the mainstream. Nature and seasonal changes will play a greater part in design schemes, the use and layout of a space will become progressively flexible, and technological developments will allow the designer greater scope than ever: a fireplace without the need for a flue or a portable, self-contained office space that can be assembled in the time it takes a microwave to defrost a TV dinner.

Despite all of this, quality and beauty will still be of paramount importance, and good design will continue to strike a balance between the past and the future.

The 21st century will not be mystical. It will be very human.
Philippe Starck (French) – designer

Glossary

Acetate Clear, plastic film in sheets or rolls that is used for overlays.

Achromatic colours Black, white and grey: 'pure' neutrals that are devoid of hue. They are added to hues to create tonal variations.

Acrylic paint Similar to watercolour paint but with a plastic binder.

Advancing colours Strongly saturated colours (red, orange, yellow, etc.) that appear to bring surfaces closer to the eye. Also known as 'warm' colours.

Analogous colours Closely related colours that are neighbours on the colour wheel – yellow, yellow-green, green and blue-green, for example.

Art deco Design style of the 1920s and 1930s (named after the 1925 *Exposition des Arts Décoratifs et Industriels Modernes* in Paris) heavily influenced by cubist art and contemporary mechanical forms.

Art nouveau Late nineteenth-century style of art and architecture that was opposed to the classicism of the immediate past.

Arts and Crafts Movement Late nineteenth-century group of artists who advocated a revival of traditional craftsmanship and pre-industrial values.

Axis The imaginary straight line passing through a figure, facade, ground plan, or pictorial or sculptural composition about which the main parts are arranged so as to give an impression of balance.

Axonometric A two-dimensional, scaled projection drawn directly from plan that gives a three-dimensional effect without using any perspective.

Baroque Rich European style of architecture and decoration, popular during the seventeenth and eighteenth centuries and characterized by a theatrical use of ornamentation and grandeur.

Bauhaus Design school based in Germany during the 1920s that sought to dismantle the barriers separating decorative art and engineering.

Beaux-arts In architecture, an academic and eclectic style of the nineteenth and twentieth centuries practised by graduates of the Beaux Arts School, Paris, and following the same principles.

Brief A list of the client's planning and/or decorating requirements.

Building regulations A national book of regulations designed to maintain building standards.

Chair rail *See* Dado rail.

Circulation The way that people move around a space: the flow in, out and through a space.

Classical Architectural and decorative stylistic motifs prevalent in the designs of Greek or Roman antiquity.

Colour wheel A circular depiction of the primary, secondary and tertiary colours, arranged clockwise in spectral order and beginning and ending with red.

Complementary colours Pairs of colours that occupy directly opposing positions on the colour wheel and that produce grey when mixed together: red and green, blue and orange, yellow and purple, for example. In use, they are dynamically contrasting.

Computer-Aided Design (CAD) Computer programs that allow users to set up their drawings on-screen, enabling them to work faster and with greater flexibility and to make required adjustments with ease.

Concept board Presentation board used to convey the mood and character of a scheme.

Cool colours *See* Receding colours.

Dado Beading or panelling fixed on the lower portion of the wall above the skirting board.

Dado rail A wooden or plaster moulding fixed horizontally to the wall traditionally used to prevent the backs of chairs from damaging walls. Also called a chair rail.

Damp-proof course (DPC) A layer of asphalt, lead, slate, zinc, plastic, polythene, copper, or any other impervious material, laid in a wall above ground level to prevent rising damp.

Decorative specification A written instruction to a decorator setting out the types, colours and codes of paint or wallpaper to be used in a room with precise instructions for preparation of surfaces.

Downlighter Recessed or ceiling-mounted fittings that throw light downwards.

Earth colours Oxide pigments that are made from refined clays and minerals dug from the ground. Available as powders or liquids.

Elevation A drawing made by projection onto a vertical plane.

Ergonomic design Workable plans and layouts that are based on the accepted measurements of space needed for human functions and requirements.

Georgian style A style of architecture and decoration associated with the 'four Georges' in England (George I, II, III and IV, 1714–1830). Combines renaissance, rococo and neoclassical elements, with classicism predominating in some forms.

Glasgow school Term applied to group of late nineteenth- and early twentieth-century artists led by Charles Rennie Mackintosh which produced a distinctive Scottish version of art nouveau.

Gothic Architectural style of twelfth-century French origin, widely adopted throughout Western Europe.

Gouache Opaque, water-based paint, in which the pigments are bound with glue or gum arabic.

Graphics Illustrations, diagrams or designs accompanying printed matter.

Grey An achromatic colour, intermediate in lightness between white and black and decoratively neutral.

Hi-tech Industrially inspired style of design, including wire-grid shelving and steel.

Holistic design Consideration of the role the senses play in interior design, including smell, sound, the tactile quality of materials specified, and the psychological effects of different colours and levels of light.

Hue The pure colour, relating to the spectrum. All colours are similar to one, or a proportion of two, of the spectral hues: red, orange, yellow, green, blue, indigo and violet. Physically, hue is determined by wavelength.

Indigo A deep, moody blue on the red side of the spectrum.

Industrial design The application of aesthetic and practical criteria to the design of machine-made articles from the mid-nineteenth century onwards, in the hope of creating a marriage between the two.

Intensity Synonym for saturation.

Interior decoration The decoration of a room to include the surfaces, furniture, furnishings and display of art and decorative objects.

Interior decorator Advises clients on the layout, furnishing and decoration of a given space and will supervise a project if required.

Isometric A two-dimensional, scaled projection that gives a three-dimensional effect without the use of perspective. It differs from an axonometric in that the original plan has to be redrawn at an angle before the projection can be executed.

Jacobean style Style of architecture and decoration prevalent in England during the reign of James I (1603–25). In interiors, there is much use of elaborate plasterwork and wood carving.

Lamp The modern word for a bulb, particularly referring to low-voltage lamps, which are very small.

Landscape format A painting, drawing, etc. which is wider than it is high. So called because most representations of landscape have this shape.

Lightness The dimension of a surface colour falling between white and black, through an intermediate series of greys. Sometimes referred to as value – the amount of light a colour sample appears to reflect. The measure of how white or black, light or dark a colour appears.

Light fitting An appliance that provides support and electrical connection to a lamp (bulb) or lamps (bulbs). It often incorporates the means of controlling the light – by a shade, for example.

Lighting plan Plan and key (often executed as an overlay on a furniture layout) showing type and position of light fittings to be used and position of sockets and switches.

Mannerism Term coined in the twentieth century to describe the European art of the period 1515–1610. Typified by stylistic trickery and bizarre effects.

Minimalism A style stripped of all unnecessary decoration.

Modernism A style that developed in the fine and applied arts in the early twentieth century, based on a rejection of traditional approaches in favour of more industrial, unornamented genres.

Monochromatic Although literally meaning 'containing only one colour', in decorating terms, it describes a scheme based around a single colour family.

Neoclassical style Restrained style that emerged as a reaction to the excesses of rococo style in the second half of the eighteenth century. Characterized by simple, geometrical forms and the sparing use of Greek and Roman architectural ornament.

Neutral Non-colour. The 'true' neutrals are black, white and grey, but beiges, creams, off-whites and so forth are 'accepted' neutrals, as are natural materials, such as wood and stone.

One-point perspective Design illustration used to show how a completed space will look. The perspective effect is created by reducing the height of three-dimensional objects and spaces as they become more distant. Unlike a two-point perspective, it is based on just one vanishing point.

Order In classical architecture, a column with base, shaft, capital and entablature decorated and proportioned to one of the accepted modes: Doric, Tuscan, Ionic, Corinthian or Composite.

Palladianism Architectural movement that flourished in England around 1720–70, taking its inspiration from the sixteenth century Venetian architect Andrea Palladio.

Pantone A type of felt-tipped, marker pen that conforms to the convention of Pantone colours. Used for colour-rendering and to produce a subtle, contemporary effect.

Pastel Dry pigment bound with gum and used in stick form for drawing. A fixative is used to make it adhere to the ground.

Pastels In decorating, the soft, white added tints of a colour. When expressed as pastels, colours which would normally contrast when fully saturated are reconciled.

Perspective The method of representing a three-dimensional object or a particular volume of space on a flat or nearly flat surface.

Plan The horizontal disposition of the parts of a building and also a drawing or diagram showing this, as seen from above.

Planning permission Official approval and permission which must be given by the local authority before certain types of building/decorating work can take place.

Portrait format A painting, drawing etc., which is higher than it is wide.

Primary colours Red, blue and yellow: the three pure, unmixed colours from which all others are derived, and which cannot themselves be produced by any mixture.

Procurement schedule A list of items required for purchase on a room-by-room basis including required delivery or installation dates.

Purity (of colour) A synonym for saturation.

Receding colours The shorter-wavelength colours, such as blue, green and violet, which appear to move away from the eye, giving an impression of distance and space. Also known as 'cool' colours.

Regency English decorative style that absorbed a wide range of contemporary continental influences. Popular during the early nineteenth century.

Renaissance The classically inspired revival of European arts and letters which began in Italy in the fourteenth century.

Rococo Exuberant, early eighteenth-century European style characterized by scalloped curves.

Rustic Frivolous eighteenth-century style of decoration applied to both roughly hewn, outdoor furniture and interior plasterwork. Now often used to describe a simple 'country style' interior.

Sample board An attractively mounted board that shows a proposed colour scheme and actual samples of materials for decorating a room. It should show a realistic picture of a scheme for an individual room.

Saturation The term used to describe the strength or vividness of a colour, the extent to which a particular red, for example, impresses the viewer by its redness. High saturation indicates a pure colour; low saturation a greyed one.

Scale plan Floor plans of a room or space drawn to scale.

Schedule of works A list of the order and type of required works on a room-by-room basis, including demolition, structural, lighting, electrical and surface decoration work.

Secondary colours Orange, green and purple: the colours resulting from an equal mixture of two primaries.

Section A representation of a vertical slice through a wall, providing a view of an interior space and used to show two or more separate areas that are divided by walls and the relationship between them.

Shade In common usage, a colour differing slightly from a specified hue or colour (for example, a 'shade of blue' or 'a greyish-green shade'). Technically, a term used to define degrees of lightness, indicating a pure colour that has been mixed with black.

Shaker Named after an American sect founded in 1747. Shaker furniture is typified by its functional design and lack of ornament.

Sketch A rough preliminary version of a composition.

Skirting board Edging, usually made of wood, fixed around interior walls at floor level to protect the walls from knocks and scuffs.

Soil pipe Vertical pipe, ventilated at the top, which carries sewage into the soil drain and then to the sewer.

Spectrum The coloured image formed when white light is spread out, according to its wavelength, by being passed through a prism. The relative intensities of the colours in the spectrum of, say, artificial light will differ from those of sunlight.

Survey An exercise in which detailed, accurate measurements of a room are taken and recorded and from which a plan is then drawn up to scale. All physical details of the space are also noted.

Swatch Small piece of material or card used as a sample.

Task light A light fitting used for a specific, localized function.

Tertiary colour Colour between a primary and a secondary colour on the colour wheel or the intermediate colour resulting from a mixture of two secondary colours.

Tint A colour of pigment containing a large amount of white, referred to in decorating as a pastel. In common usage, a colour appearing to modify another weakly ('beige with a pink tint', for example).

Tonal values The gradations of one colour from light to dark. Pink is a light value (or tint) of red, while maroon is a dark value (or shade).

Tone Technically, a term used to define degrees of lightness, including a pure colour that has been mixed with grey. In common usage, a synonym for lightness, a colour differing slightly from a specified colour ('a tone of green'), or a colour that appreciably modifies another ('green with bluish tone', for example).

Traffic flow The number of pairs of feet and the lanes and direction of 'traffic' which pass across a floor, and which must be considered when planning furniture positions or selecting flooring.

Two-point perspective Design illustration in which the effect of perspective is achieved by reducing the height of three-dimensional objects and spaces as they become more distant. It is based on two vanishing points and produces a more realistic result than the one-point perspective.

Upholsterer A specialist in furnishing with textiles and upholstering furniture.

Uplighter A light fitting that projects light up onto a ceiling, sending reflected light back down.

Value A synonym for lightness when applied to colour or tone.

Virtual-reality design Computer programs that allow the designer to execute three-dimensional drawings and to add sounds, animation and titling to create an interactive presentation.

Wallwasher A light fitting that directs the light from a recessed fitting in the ceiling on to a wall or items placed on the wall

Warm colours *See* Advancing colours.

Watercolour Water-soluble pigments combined with water-soluble gum as a binder and water as a medium, used to make transparent paint.

Working drawing A detailed drawing illustrating the specific requirements for bespoke furniture or joinery.

Further reading

Books

Chapter 1

Norman Foster and Martin Pawley, *A Global Architecture*, Universe Publishing (incorporated division of Rizzoli), New York, 1999

Peter Thornton, *Authentic Decor: The Domestic Interior 1620–1920*, Weidenfeld & Nicolson, London, 1984

John Styles and Michael Snodin, *Design and the Decorative Arts in Britain* (4 volumes), V&A Publications, London, 2004

Owen Jones, *The Grammar of Ornament*, Dorling Kindersley, London, 2001

Charles McCorquodale , *The History of Interior Decoration*, Phaidon Press, Oxford, 1988

Simon Jervis (ed.), *Dictionary of Design and Designers*, Penguin Reference Books, Harmondsworth, 1984

Charlotte and Peter Fiell, *Design of the 20th Century*, Taschen, London/Köln, 2001

Chapter 2

Ashley Hicks and Tom Ford, *David Hicks*, Scriptum Editions, London, 2002

Chapter 3

Selwyn Goldsmith, *Designing for the Disabled: The New Paradigm*, Architectural Press, Oxford, 1997

Roger Banks Pye, *Inspirational Interiors* (aka *Colefax & Fowler: New Inspirations*), Ryland Peters & Small, London, 1997

Thomas C. Mitchell, *New Thinking in Design: Conversations in Theory and Practice*, Van Nostrand Reinhold, London, 1996

Patricia Rodeman, *Patterns in Interior Environments: Perception, Psychology, and Practice*, John Wiley & Sons, London/New York, 1999

Kevin McCloud, *Kevin McCloud's Lighting Book: The Ultimate Guide to Lighting Every Room in the Home*, Ebury Press, London, 1995

Sally Storey, *Lighting: Recipes and Ideas, Simple Solutions for the Home*, Quadrille, London, 2003

Tom Porter and Sue Goodman, *Design Drawing Techniques for Architects, Graphic Designers and Artists*, Butterworth Architecture, Oxford, 1992

Gary Gordon and James L Knuckolls , *Interior Lighting for Designers*, John Wiley & Sons, New York, 1995

Chapter 4

The Colour Book, Mitchell Beazley, London, 1997

Morton Walker, *The Power of Colour*, B. Jain Publishers, India, 2002

Mary C. Miller, *Color for Interior Architecture*, John Wiley & Sons, New York, 1997

Catherine Merrick and Rebecca Day, *The Curtain Design Directory*, Merrick & Day, Gainsborough, 1999

Caroline Clifton Mogg and Melanie Paine, *The Curtain Book*, Mitchell Beazley, London 1988

Melanie Paine, *The New Fabric Magic*, Francis Lincoln, London, 1988

Barty Phillips, *Fabrics and Wallpapers*, Ebury Press, London, 1991

Florence M. Montgomery, *Textiles in America 1650–1870*, John Wiley & Sons, New York/Chichester, 1984

Laurie Williamson, *The Complete Book of Flooring*, The Crowood Press, Marlborough, 2004

Judy Juracek, *Surfaces: Visual Research for Artists, Architects and Designers*, Thames & Hudson, London, 1996

Chapter 5

William L. Wilkoff, *Practicing Universal Design: An interpretation of the ADA*, Van Nostrand Reinhold, New York, 1994

Patricia K. Gilbert, *Successful Interior Projects Through Effective Contract Documents*, RS Means Co, Kingston, MA, 1995

Mary V. Knackstedt, *The Interior Designer Business Handbook: A Complete Guide to Profitability*, JohnWiley & Sons, New York/Chichester, 2002

Mary V. Knackstedt, *Interior Design and Beyond*, John Wiley & Sons, New York/Chichester, 2002

Christine Peitrowski, *Professional Practice for Interior Designers*, Van Nostrand Reinhold, New York, 1994

Chapter 6

Edith Cherry, *Programming for Design: From Theory to Practice*, John Wiley & Sons, New York/ Chichester, 1999

Chapter 7

Sara O'Marberry, *Innovations in Health Care Design*, Van Nostrand Reinhold, New York, 1995

Robert L. Alderman, *How to Prosper as an Interior Designer: A Business and Legal Guide,* John Wiley & Sons, New York/Chichester, 1997

Julie K. Rayfield, *The Office Interior Design Guide: An Introduction for Facilities Managers*, John Wiley & Sons, New York/Chichester, 1997

James E. Rappaport, Karen Daroff and Robert Cushman, *Office Planning and Design Desk Reference*, John Wiley & Sons, New York/Chichester, 1992

Michael J Lopez, *Retail Store Planning and Design Manual*, National Retail Federation, 1986

Jeremy Myerson and Philip Ross, *The Creative Office*, Laurence King Publishing, London 2002

Rashid Din, *New Retail*, Conran Octopus, London 2000

UK periodicals and magazines

BBC Homes & Antiques
Country Homes & Interiors
Elle Décor
Elle Decoration
Grand Designs
Homes & Gardens
House & Garden
IDFX
The English Home
Wallpaper
World of Interiors

US periodicals and magazines

Architecture Magazine
Architectural Digest
Architectural Lighting
Better Homes & Gardens
Canadian House & Home
Canadian Interiors
Contract Magazine
Elle Decor
Hospitality Design
House Beautiful
Interior Design Magazine
Interiors and Sources
Metropolis Magazine
Restaurant Hospitality
Southern Accents
Sunset Magazine
Traditional Home

Relevant magazines can also be accessed online through www.dezignare.com, www.condenet.com and www.magsonthenet.com

Useful addresses in the UK

The British Interior Design Association
3/18 Chelsea Habour Design Centre
Chelsea Harbour
London
SW10 OXE
Tel: +44 (0)20 7349 0800
Email: enquiries@bida.org
www.bida.org
Lists 150 interior designers across the UK.

The Chartered Society of Designers
5 Bermondsey Exchange
179-181 Bermondsey Street
London
SE1 3UW
Tel: +44 (0)20 7357 8088
www.csd.org.uk
The Chartered Society of Designers provides a
range of services for members, including a list of
recruitment companies, but is mainly aimed at
experienced designers.

The Design Council
34 Bow Street
London
WC2E 7DL
Tel: +44 (0)20 7420 5200
Email: info@designcouncil.org.uk
www.designcouncil.org.uk
www.yourcreativefuture.co
The Design Council's introductory guide to careers
in design features links to a few interior designers'
websites and a case study interview with an interior
designer.

The Design Directory
European Design Innovations Ltd
PO Box 421
St. Albans
Herts
AL1 5FB
Tel: +44 (0)1727 837874
Email: edi@dial.pipex.co
www.designdirectory.co.uk
Provides listings of potential employers, featuring
hotlinks to employer websites. (Also check lists
under 'architectural design').

London Enterprise Agency (LENTA)
4 Snow Hill
London
EC1A 2BS
Tel: +44 (0)20 7236 3000
Fax: +44 (0)20 7329 0226
Email: lenta.ventures@lentA.co.uk
A consortium of companies and the Corporation of
London dedicated to developing small businesses
and education projects and providing financial
advice.

The Prince's Trust
18 Park Square East
London
NW1 4LH
Tel: +44 (0)800 842 842
Head Office: +44 (0)20 7543 1234
www.princes-trust.org.ik
Provides help for young people wishing to set up
their own businesses.

The Royal Institute of British Architects
66 Portland Place
London
W1B 1AD
Tel: +44 (0)20 7580 5533
Email: info@inst.riba.org
www.riba.org.uk
Lists around 300 registered architectural practices
with interior design specialisms.

Shell LiveWIRE
Shell UK Limited
Hawthorn House
Forth Banks
Newcastle upon Tyne
NE1 3SG
Tel: +44 (0)845 757 3252
www.shell-livewire.org
Competitive awards scheme, advice and training on
business start-ups for young people.

www.architecture.com
In association with *The Architects Journal*, advertises
vacancies from a wide range of occupations in the
construction industry, including interior design.

www.biat.org.uk
The website of the British Institute of Architectural
Technologists and worth checking out for opportu-
nities in related areas.

www.careersinconstruction.com
Lists hundreds of jobs in the construction industry,
including posts for architects, designers, architectural assistants and contractors.

www.design-week.co.uk
Job seekers can register free to browse for a trial
period *Design Week* magazine where some vacancies
are advertised. Search under 'concept designer',
'visual merchandiser' or 'theme designer'. Also good
for finding out what is happening in the industry,
including new contracts and developments.

www.ifiworld.org
Website of the International Federation of Interior
Architects and Designers (IFI), promoting the
worldwide exchange of information related to the
interior design profession.

www.interiordesignhandbook.com
Provides lists of possible contacts and employers.

www.newdesignpartners.com
An online directory in association with *Design Week*
magazine providing contact details of UK companies, work undertaken, clients and recent projects.

www.rec.uk.com
Lists a number of recruitment agencies that specialize in interior design. At the time of writing, there
are eleven agencies listed in the UK at this site, but
bear in mind that agencies do tend to prefer experienced designers.

www.yell.com
Provides listings under 'interior designers', but also
under 'refurbishment', 'commercial premises',
'computer-aided design' and 'office fitters'.

Useful addresses in the US

American Society of Interior Designers (ASID)
608 Massachusetts Avenue NE
Washington DC
20002 – 6006
Tel: +1 (202) 546 3480
www.asid.org
The leading professional organization for interior designers in the US. Promotes professionalism in interior design services and conducts independent research on related topics.

Ecosmart
318 Seaboard Lane,
Suite 208
Franklin
TN37067
Tel: +1 (615) 261 7300
www.ecosmart.com
Uses state-of-the-art technology and natural resources to increase quality. Runs seminars and symposiums.

Environmental Building News
BuildingGreen Inc
122 Birge Street
Suite 30
Brattleboro
VT 0530
Tel: +1 (802) 257 7300
www.buildingreen.com
Provides online newsletter, including order catalogue of 1,200 green design products, checklists and technical information.

Foundation for Interior Design Education Research (FIDER)
146 Monroe Center NW
Suite 318
Grand Rapids
MI49503-2822
Tel: +1 (616) 458 0400
www.fider.org
Sets standards for post-secondary design education, evaluates college and university interior design programmes and publishes a list of accredited programmes.

Green Seal
1001 Connecticut Avenue NW
Suite 827
Washington DC 20036 –5525
Tel: +1 (202) 872 6400
www.greenseal.org
Green Seal is a non-profit organization awarding the Green Seal of Approval to environmentally responsible products and services.

Interior Design Educators Council (IDEC)
7150 Winton Drive
Suite 300
Indianapolis
1N46268
Tel: +1 317 328 4437
info@idec.org www.idec.org
Includes a list of interior design schools and announcements related to education.

International Interior Design Association (IIDA)
IIDA Headquarters
13-500 Merchandise Mart
Chicago
IL 60654
Tel: +1 (313) 467 1950
www.iida.org,
A professional networking and educational association committed to enhancing the quality of life through excellence in interior design.

National Council of Interior Design Qualifications (NCIDQ)
1200 18th Street NW
Suite 1001
Washington DC
2003-2506
Tel: +1 (202) 721 0220
www.ncidq.org
Serves to identify to the public those interior designers who have met the minimum standards for professional practice through its examination.

Small Business Association
26 Federal Plaza
Suite 3100
New York,
NY10278
Tel: +1 (212) 264 4354
Fax +1 (212) 264 4963
This association can supply useful information for anyone considering the possibility of setting up a small design practice in the US.

US Green Building Council
1015 18th Street NW
Suite 508,
Washington DC
20036
Tel: +1 (202) 828 7422
www.usgbc.org
The US Green Building Council is the US building industry's only balanced, non-profit-making coalition promoting 'Green Building' policies, programmes, technologies, standards and practices.

www.auid.org
Website of the Association of University Interior Designers (AUID), promoting the discussion of issues related to interior design work at universities and institutes of higher education.

www.dezignare.com
Has a 'student corner' with announcements and answers to questions, as well as information on schools and other learning resources.

www.greendesign.net
The website for Green Design Network, focusing on building and design concerns.

www.headhunter.net
Focuses on experienced professionals looking to move jobs.

www.interiordesignjobs.com
Contains information about career opportunities and related news sources.

www.internweb.com
Provides information about applying for internships as well as postgraduate positions and other career information.

www.jobnext.com
Offers helpful information about creating a résumé (CV), interviewing techniques and also includes job listings.

www.oikos.com
The website for Green Building Source, providing information about green conferences and including a product gallery, database and library.

www.resumesandcoverletters.com
Offers tips on how to create résumés (CVs) and covering letters and includes a page of links to additional career resources and sites.

Index

Page numbers in **bold** refer to illustrations

A

accent colours 100
accent lighting 83
accessories and details 118, 119
Ackerman, Rudolph 20
acoustics 105
activities, catering for 64, 67, 74
Adam, Robert 17
    Kenwood House, England **103**
Africa 34
after-sales manuals 139
ageing society issue 154
amenities:
    blurring of functions 176–7
    new types of 176
America *see* United States
American Bar, Vienna **23**
American colonial style 101
'anthropometrics' 67
approvals and permissions 132–3
architects 10
Armani, Giorgio 30
art deco 24
art nouveau 20
Arts and Crafts Movement 20
associations, professional 164, 177
asymmetry 37, 70
Australia 175
Austria 16, 20
AutoCAD 90
axonometric projections 91, **92**, **163**

B

BAC (British Accreditation Council) 146
balance 72
baroque style 14, 16, 17
Bauhaus 24, 97
Beaux Arts style 20, 24
bed and window treatments 113, 116
Belgium 20
Berlin 17
Bernini, Gianlorenzo: St Peter's, Rome: canopy **15**
brief, taking 44–5, 124–5
British Accreditation Council (BAC) 146
budgets 45
building regulations 76
buildings:
    need for construction knowledge 74, 75
    fabric of 46–7
Burlington, Lord 17
business cards 152, 159

C

CAD (Computer-Aided Design):
    CAD operator opportunities **173**

and design education 154
and flooring design **110**, 111
hand-rendering 90
and office design 174
potential dangers of 89
presentation packages 122
producing the design 89–90, **89**
producing visuals **179**
cameras 46
Campbell, Nina 29, 30
career options 166–74
Casa Calvert, Barcelona: hall (Gaudí) **21**
cave paintings 6
CDM (Construction Design Management) 137
ceilings 48
Charles II, king of England 16
Charlottenburg Palace, Munich (Nering) **15**
Chauvet caves, Ardèche Valley, France **6**
Chermayeff, Serge 24
China 72, 175, 176
Chippendale, Thomas 20
circulation 45, 74
City & Guilds 147
Claridges Hotel, London: foyer **59**
classical orders of architecture 69, **69**
classical style 68, 70
client/designer relationship 40–4
clients:
    acceptance of supplies 136
    and contractors 132, 137
    identifying client's needs 40, 43–4, 57
    input of client's own ideas 36, 43, 124
    interpreting client's identity 38
    obtaining client agreement 130
    presentations to 122, 128–30
    proposal to 125–6
    taking the brief 44–5, 124–5
Colony Club, New York (de Wolfe) **23**
colour 96–104
    accent colours 100
    colour associations 101
    colour trends 104
    and mood 98–9
    period colour 101
    psychology of 100–1
    and sense of space 105
    and texture 106
colour perception 103–4
colour wheel 97
commercial interior design:
    areas of specialization 26, 166–74
    as business enhancement 38
    as career option 166
    colour psychology 101
    company logo creation 30
    main areas of activity 26
    need for teamwork 145
commercial projects:

circulation requirement 45, 74
construction design management (CDM) 137
consulting with key staff 43, 45
fire officer involvement 133
health officer involvement 133
programming and phasing 43
taking the brief 45
communication:
    and international projects 31, 90
    and the project team 135
    services for 85
    web-based project hubs 136
    when phasing a project 43
company images 30
completion/handover 139–40
Computer-Aided Design *see* CAD (Computer-Aided Design)
computers:
    and design education 154
    as main design tool **173**
    production of graphics 88
    and project phasing 43
    see also CAD (Computer-Aided Design)
concept boards 60–1, 62, 127
    examples **10**, **30**, **34**, **60–1**, **66**, **127**, **162**, **169**
concept sketch **162**
concepts, formulating 58, 62, 127
Conran, Terence 24
    Plateau, Canary Wharf **23**
conservation areas 133
Construction Design Management (CDM) 137
consultant fees 140
'contemporary classic' style 58
contractors:
    as client's employees 132, 137
    selecting 131, 132
    supply of estimates 132
    and working drawings 130, 132
contrast 73
    of accessories 118
    textural contrast 104, 106–7
'country house' look 24
courses in design:
    application route 147
    assessment 152, 154
    basic strategy of 149
    course content 148–52
    entry requirements 145, 147–8
    selecting a course 145–7
    typical curriculum 148
Crace & Co 20
Craftsman style 20
creativity and concept 127
curtains 116
CVs 159
    accompanying letter 160–1
    content and presentation 160

CV checklist 158
enhancing through placements 161

D

datum 70
David Schefer Design: restaurant,
    Philadelphia 33
De Architectura (Vitruvius) 69
decorative schemes:
    decorative specification 130
    developing a scheme 104–5
    and texture 106–7
Decorex trade fair, London: stand design 168
design analyses 124–5
design courses *see* courses in design
design education:
    complementary education 146
    future of 154–5
    role of 154
design history *see* history of design
design illustration *see* illustrating designs
design practices:
    European 30
    sizes and types of 29, 30
    United States 30
design, principles of 66–73
designs, drawing up 86–91
details and accessories 118, 119
de Wolfe, Elsie 24
    Colony Club, New York 23
disabled users 74
district surveyors 9, 133
diversification 29
doors:
    door furniture 118, 119
    surveying 50
Dorchester Hotel, London 54
Dos Aguas Palace, Valencia 16
drawings:
    design illustration 90–4
    drawing up designs 86–91
    working drawings 91

E

eco-friendly environments 155
ecology 154
educational establishment design 172
education, design *see* design education
eighteenth-century design 16–20
electrics 50
elevations 63, 87, 89
emailing 90
Empire style 20
employment, finding:
    applying for jobs 160–1
    career options 166–74
    choosing a direction 159, 160
    creating a website 160

the interview 164
opportunities 174
overview 157–9
your first job 164
see also CVs
Endell, August 20
energy consumption 154
England 16, 17
entertainment centres 170
entertainment, home 85
entertainment and hospitality design 168, 169
environment:
    creating healthy environments 64
    eco-friendly environments 155
ergonomics 68
Erskine, Ralph: house, Stockholm 31
estate agents 166
estimates and tenders 131, 132
event design 174
exhibition design 166, 168
expenses 141
experimentation 38
*Exposition des Arts Décoratifs et Industriels
    Modernes, L'* 24
extensions 134

F

fees 140–1
feng shui 72
'Fibonacci sequence' 68
FIDER (The Foundation for Interior Design
    Education Research) 146
finishes and materials 108–16
fire officers 9, 133
fireplaces 48
fire-retardancy 108
fixed fee 141
flooring:
    glass panels in 76, 77
    ordering individual designs 110–11
    surveying 50
floor treatments 108–9
focal points 73
Fontaine, Pierre-François-Léonard 17, 20
Fowler, John 24
France 14, 16, 17
    period colours 101
Frank, Jean-Michel 24
freehand perspectives 62
freehand sketching 91–2
freelance illustrators 91
furniture:
    developing layouts 88
    enhancing space with 76
    placement of 117
    selecting 116–17
    using scale templates 88, 88, 128
future of industry 175–7

G

Gabriel, Ange-Jacques 16
Gaudí, Antoni 20
    Casa Calvert, Barcelona: hall 21
Germany 16, 17, 20
global influences 30
globalization 31–4, 175–6, 177
'golden section' 68
graduate shows 152, 152
Grafton, Ann 25
Gran Hotel Domine, Bilbao 35
graphics 30, 88
Gray, Eileen 24
    Roquebrune, France 22
grid patterns 72
Gropius, Walter 24

H

Hamburg, Germany: shopping emporium 33
Hampton Court Palace 16
handover *see* completion/handover
haute couture approach 177
healthcare design 172
health officers 133
health and safety 137
heating:
    fundamentals of 76, 79
    surveying 50
Henry IV, king of France
Hepplewhite, George 17, 20
Hicks, David 24
HI Hotel, Nice: lobby 170
historical study:
    and design courses 149
    value of 14
history of design:
    seventeenth century 14–16
    eighteenth century 16–20
    nineteenth century 20–1, 24
    twentieth century 22–3, 24–5
holistic design 64, 100, 154, 180
Holland 16, 17
home entertainment 85
Homewood House, Baltimore 103
Hong Kong 176
Hope, Thomas 17, 20
Hoppen, Kelly 30
horizontal lines 72
Horta, Victor 20
hospitality and entertainment design 168, 170–1
hotel design 170
Houghton Hall: white drawing room (Kent) 18
housing developments 27
Hubbard, Elbert 20
human dimensions 67

I

illustrating designs 91–4

rendering techniques 92–3, 94
implementation 130
Inspirational Household Furniture and Decoration
     (Hope) **17**, 20
inspiration, seeking 62
installation 137
insurance 177
interior decoration 145
interior decorators 179
interior designer/architects 26
interior designers:
     diversification into related areas **29**, 30
     educational requirements 145
     general perception of 26
     global exchange of ideas 31
     licensing of 154–6
     need for professionalism 26
     qualities needed 8, 144–5
     rise of 'signature designers' 177
     role of 8, 42–3
     working with other professionals 9–10, 43
interior design profession:
     future of 175–7
     need to define itself 177, 179
     planning a career in: *chart* 178
International Federation of Interior Designers 148
Internet:
     online design courses 154
     as source of suppliers 106
internships 161, 164
invoices 139, 141
isometric projections 91, **92**
Italy 14, 17, 20
Itten, Johannes 97

J
Japan 154, 175, 176, 179
Japanese bathroom 70
Jefferson, Thomas 20
jobs, finding *see* employment, finding
joinery 50
Jones, Inigo 16
     Queen's House, Greenwich **15**
Juvarra, Filippo 16

K
Kelmscott House, England: bedroom (Morris) **21**
ken (Japanese measurement) 69–70
Kent, William 17
     Houghton Hall: white drawing room **18**
Kenwood House, England (Adam) **103**
kitchens:
     design specialization 27
     modular units for 88

L
La Cartuja, Granada: sacristy **19**
La Granja, Royal Palace of 16

Lancaster, Nancy 24
Lauren, Ralph 30
Le Brun, Charles 14, 16
     Hall of Mirrors, Versailles **15**
Le Corbusier 24, 70
     Villa Savoye, France **23**
Le Vau, Louis 14
libraries, trade reference *see* trade reference
     libraries
lifelong learning 155
light:
     and colour perception 103–4
     enhancing 76
     global variation 31, 34
     orientation of 46–7
light fittings 79, 80–1, 83
lighting:
     accent lighting 83
     flexibility and control 83–4
     general lighting 83
     and hospitality design **170**
     lighting plans 89, **89**, 122, **131**
     preparing specification/plan 79
     task lighting 83
lines 72
listed buildings 133
litigation 177
local authorities 132
Loos, Adolf: Müller House, Prague (Loos)
     98, **110**
Louis III, king of France
Louis XIV, king of France 14
Lupino, Barcelona **45**

M
Mackintosh, Charles Rennie 20
Madrid, Royal Palace of 16
maintenance manuals 139
Malmaison, Le, Paris (Percier/Fontaine) **19**
Mann Residence, California **117**
Mansart, François 14
Marot, Daniel 16
materials and finishes 108–16
mature students 147
measuring and surveying *see* surveying and
     measuing
mechanical engineers 10
media, role of 35–6
medically orientated design 172
Mendelsohn, Eric 24
Messel, Oliver **54**
Middle East 27, 176
Mies van der Rohe, Ludwig 24
     Tugendhat House, Brno **22**
MiniCAD 90
minimalism 58, **59**, 177
Miralles, Enric **58**
mirrors 76, 77

modernism 24
Modular, le 70
Monticello, Virginia (Jefferson) 20
mood and colour 98–9
Morris, William 20
     Kelmscott House, England: bedroom **21**
Morse-Libby Mansion, Portland, ME **21**
Müller House, Prague (Loos) **98**, **110**
Musée d'Art Contemporain, Bordeaux (Putman)
     118

N
Napoleon I, emperor of France 20
NCIDQ (National Council for Interior Design
     Qualification) 156
neoclassical style 17, 20
     associated colours 101, **103**
Nering, Arnold: Charlottenburg Palace, Munich
     15
networking 157, 159
Neumann, Johann Balthasar 16
     Residenz, Würzburg: staircase **19**
neutral colours 97, 100
Newton, Sir Isaac 97
Nike Pavilion, London **29**
nineteenth-century design 20–1, 24
     associated colours 101

O
office design 172, 174
     ergonomic design **67**
     home offices 84, 174
     'hot-desking' 67
     specializing in 11
OFSTED (Office for Standards in Education)
     147
ordering principles 70, 72–3
orders (classical) of architecture 69, **69**
oriental proportions 69–70

P
Pacific Rim 176
paints 111
Palladian revival 17
Palladio, Andrea 17, 69
     Villa Rotunda, Vicenza **69**
Paris 24
patronage 14, 20
pattern 107
Percier, Charles **17**, 20
period colour 101
permissions and approvals 132–3
perspective sketches **63**, 91, 93, **129**, **163**
pets **40**
Philadelphia, USA: restaurant (David Schefer
     Design) **33**
placements 161, 164
planning and design 128

practical planning 74–6
planning officers 9, 132–3
planning permission 134
plans 128, **128**, **163**
    method of execution 86–7, **86–7**
    working drawings 91
Plateau, Canary Wharf (Conran) **23**
Poiret, Paul 24
portfolios:
    and design course interview 147
    as employment aid 152, 160, 161
    putting together 161, 162–3
    showing to client 44
Portugal 176
practical planning 74–6
preparation 136
presentations:
    CAD packages 122
    preparing for 122, 128, 130
    presentation aids **129**
principles of design 66–73
procurement schedules 136
product design:
    as design opportunity 30
    and increased options 88
professional associations 164, 177
professional practice, developments in 177
professionals, collaboration with 9–10, 43
project management:
    and designers 134
    responsiblities of project managers 134–5
    as specialist area 30, 134
projects
    fees when aborted 141
    stages of 124–40, 142
proportion 68, **72**
proposals 125–6
'proxemics' (personal space) 67
psychology of colour 100–1
purchasing 118
Putman, Andrée: Musée d'Art Contemporain,
    Bordeaux (Putman) **118**

Q

qualifications:
    certificates/diplomas 145–6, 152, 154
    degrees 145, 152, 155
    importance of 155–7
Queen's House, Greenwich (Jones) **15**
questionnaires 44

R

radial balance 70
radiator designs 79
recruitment agencies 160
Recueil de décorations intérieures (Fontaine/Percier)
    17, 20
Renaissance 14, 69

rendering techniques 92–3, **94**
repetition 73
Repository of Arts (Ackerman) 20
research, preliminary 56, 66
residential design:
    as career option 166
    domestic lifestyle challenges 26, 44
    holistic approach to 180
    home offices 84
    housing developments 27
    incorporation of technology 26, 84, 154,
        177, 180
    increasing demand for flexibility 75, 180
    influence of hospitality design 35, 36
    show houses 27
Residenz, Würzburg: staircase (Neumann) **19**
restaurants/bars:
    refurbishment of **138**
    total design of **171**
    use of colour **98**
retail charging 141
retail design 166
retention period 139–40
rhythm 73
Rocha, John 30
rococo 16
Roquebrune, France (Gray) **22**
Royal Institute of British Architects 179
Royalton Hotel, New York (Starck) **73**
rules, playing with 75–6
Russia 156, 176

S

safety 74
St Peter's, Rome: canopy (Bernini) **15**
sample boards 118, 122
    creation of 120–1
    examples **66**, **105**, **107**, **113**, **114–5**,
        116, **120–1**, **163**, **129**, **174**
Santiago de Compostela 16
scale:
    and colour 105
    principles of 68
Scandinavia 17
schedules of works 135–6
    example **135**
Schinkel, Karl Friedrich 17
sections **86**, 87, **87**
Serlio, Sebastiano 69
services:
    integrating 76, 78–85, 89
    preparing plans for 89
seventeenth-century design 14–16
Sheldon, W.J. 67
Sheraton, Thomas 20
show houses:
    design opportunities 27, 174, **175**
    as source of inspiration 56, 57

site supervision 137
sketches:
    perspective sketches 63, 91, **129**
    thumbnail sketches 122
sketching:
    and design courses 149, 150
    sketching up ideas 62, 63, 91–2
Smith, George 20
'snagging' ('punch list') stage 140
'somatotyping' 67
Soubise, Hôtel de, Paris: oval room **18**
space:
    circulation through 74
    and colour 105
    defining 75, 109
    'experiencing' when surveying 127
    illusion of **75**, 76, **76**, 105, 108
    leaving room for activities 64, 67, 74
    personal space 67
Spain 16, 17, 20
specialist publications 36
specialization 30
    career options 166–74
    commercial design 26, 166
    in decorative schemes 29
    residential design 27, 166
specifications 130–1
Starck, Philippe: Royalton Hotel, New York **73**
stencilling 111
Stern, Robert: hospital in Indiana **172**
Stickley, Gustav 20
storage 74
structural considerations 75
structural engineers 10
study, courses of *see* courses in design
Stupinigi Palace, Turin: central salon **18**
style, promotion of 30
styles:
    boundaries blurred 76
    difficulties when importing 34
    global influences on 30, 32–3, 34
    historical interpretation 57
    identifying clients' wishes 57–8
    keeping up-to-date with 56
supervision, site 136
suppliers:
    creating rapport with 106, 136
    own design services 27
    regular visits to 56
surveying and measuring 46–51, **49**, 126–7
    room checklists 48–50
    surveying a room 52–3
surveyors 9
Sweden 16
symmetry 70

T

Tagliabue, Benedetta **58**

Taliesen, Wisconsin (Wright) **22**
task lighting 83
teamwork 145
technology:
    CAD programmes 89–90
    and the design function 43, 85, 177
    and global design cooperation 31
    integrating into schemes 85
    and residential design 26, 84, 154, 177,
      180
tenders and estimates 131, 132
terminology 177, 179
texture:
    and acoustics 105
    textural contrast 104, 106–7
three-dimensions, working in 62, 90
thumbnail sketches 122
trade accounts 106
trade fairs 56
trade reference libraries:
    building up 106
    researching materials/finishes 56
    software for 154
    and specialist publications 36
traffic flow:
    checking on survey 54
    traffic-flow plans 74, 74
trends:
    colour trends 104
    influence of media 36
    sources of information 56
Tugendhat House, Brno (Mies van der Rohe)
    22
twentieth-century design 22–3, 24–5
twenty-first-century developments 26

U

UCAS route B 147
United States:
    design education 146, 147–8, 156–7
    design history 17, 20, 24
    design specialization 30
    employment opportunities 159
    interior design as norm 40
    licensing of interior designers 155–7
    listed buildings 133
    project management 134
    rise of commercial design 166
    types of interior designer 179
    viability of design industry 26
upholstered furniture 117
upholsterer/decorators 20

V

Verberckt, Jacques 16
Versace 30
Versailles, palace of 14
    Hall of Mirrors (Le Brun) **15**

vertical lines 72
Villa Rotunda, Vicenza (Palladio) **69**
Villa Savoye, France (Le Corbusier) **23**
virtual offices 174
virtual reality design **173**
visualization 174
Vitruvius 69

W

wallpaper 112
walls:
    surveying 48
    wall treatments 111–13
websites:
    as job-hunting aid 160
    web-based project hubs 136
William III and Mary II, king and queen of
    England 16
window and bed treatments 113, 116
windows:
    measuring **51**
    surveying 50
    window treatments 113, 114–15, 116
wood:
    mixing wooden furniture 116
    wood panelling 113
work experience 159
working drawings 90, **90**, 130, 132, **132**
work placements 161, 164
works, schedules of see schedules of works
Wright, Frank Lloyd 20
    Taliesen, Wisconsin **22**

Picture sources & credits

Laurence King Publishing would like to thank all
the institutions and individuals who have provided
material or artwork for use in this book.
(T=Top; B=Bottom; L=Left; R=Right)

AKG-Images, London: Joseph Martin 15BL;
    Rabatti–Domingie 17B; CDA/ Guillot
    18TR; Laurent Lecat 19TL; Erich Lessing
    23TL, 68; Robert O'Dea 69T
Amtico, Solihull, UK: 109
Arcaid, London: Richard Einzig 31 (Architect:
    Ralph Erskine); Inigo Bujedo Aguirre 35
    (Architect: Inaki Aurrecoetxea/Interior de
    signer: Javier Mariscal); Richard Bryant 48
    (Architect: G. Aitchison & Lord Leighton),
    50, 51TL (Architect: Edward Ould), 51TR
    (Interior designer: David Falla), 52/53
    (Interior designer: David Falla), 59B
    (Architect: Shideh Shaygan), 72T (Architect:
    Ed Tuttle), 73 (Interior designer: Philippe
    Starck), 75R (Architect: Eva Jiricna
    Architects), 78, 99B (Architect: Seth Stein
    Architects), 102, 173B (Architect: And-
    Associates Ltd); Ben Johnson 51B; Earl
    Carter/BELLE 54 (Architect: Greg Irvine);
    Jeremy Cockayne 55; Mark Fiennes 72B
    (Architect: Michael Graves), 119; John
    Edward Linden 117 (Architect: Fernau
    Hartman), 167 (Architect: Studio 63
    Architecture & Design); Colin Dixon 120TR;
    David Churchill 173T (Architect: GMW)
Archipress: 155
© ARS, NY and DACS, London 2004: 22TL
Laura Ashley, London: 112
Bang & Olufsen, Berkshire, UK: 85
Achim Bednorz, Cologne: 18TL
© Paul Bielenberg, Los Angeles: 166
Courtesy of Burger King: 98B
Friedrich Busam/Architekturphoto, Berlin:
    170BR
**Nina Campbell product photographed by Jamie
    Stevens, London:** 29
Claridges, London: 59T
**J. Clottes – Ministère de la Culture et de la
    Communication – Direction du Patrimoine –
    Sous Direction de L' Archéologie, France:** 6
Niall Clutton/BDG McColl: 28
Courtesy of Conran, London: Jonathan Pile
    23BL; Nicolas d'Archimbaud 171
Corbis, London: Owen Franken 15TL;
    Bettmann 19TR; Archivo Iconografico, S.A.
    21BL; G.E. Kidder Smith 21BR
Crown Paints: 99TL
Courtesy of John Cullen Lighting, London:
    80TL, 80TC, 80TR, 81, 82
Courtesy of *Daily Mail* Ideal Home, London:
    56

Andreas von Einsiedel, London: 25 (Interior designer: Ann Grafton), 33, 42 (Architect: Richard Rogers/Decoration: Anna French), 47B (Designer: Tara Bernerd), 57B, 140, 180 (Architect and interior: Chris & Joanne Pearson)

Esto, New York: Peter Aaron 172

Foscarini, Milan: 80B

Eileen Gray Archive: 22TR

Angelo Hornak, London: 15BL (Courtesy of the National Maritime Museum, Greenwich), 18B (Courtesy of The Marquess of Cholmondeley Houghton Hall, UK), 21T (Courtesy of Kelmscott Manor, Gloucestershire, UK), 103 (Courtesy of the Greater London Council)

James F. Housel: 41

David M. Joseph: 32

Peter Kent, London: 23TR © FLC/ADAGP, Paris and DACS, London 2004

Andrew Lamb: 1, 2

© **Paul M.R. Maeyaert, El Tossal, Spain:** 15TR

Duccio Malagamba, Barcelona, Spain: 58

Ignacio Martinez, Lustenau, Austria: 47T

MFI/Schreiber, UK: 27

Jonathan Moore: 84

Max Plunger, Nacka, Sweden: 7

Courtesy Andrée Putman, Paris: 118

Ellen Rapelius/Xavier Franquesa, Spain: 45

Sharrin Rees: 77

Schenk & Campbell: 75L

Pavel Stecha: 22B © DACS 2005

Pavel Stecha & Radovan Bocek, Prague: Architect Adolf Loos 98T, 110

Stencil Library, London: 49, 111

Sunley, London: 57T, 157, 175

Kozo Takayama: 67

View, London: Dennis Gilbert 9 (Architect: AHMM); Chris Gascoigne 11 (Architect: Bovis Lendlease Ltd), 71 (Architect: Thorp Design), 125 (Architect: Patel Taylor/Interior designer: Tara Bernerd), 176 (Redjacket); Fiona McLean 37; Peter Cook 100, 133 (Architect: John McAslan & Partners); Christial Michel 104 (Architect: Cardete-Huel Architectes), 170T (Architect: Matali Crasset Productions); Grant Smith 146 (Architect: Bluearc); Edmund Sumner 151 (Architect: Pringle Richards Sharratt); Paul Riddle 170BL (Architect: Edward A Stone/Interior designer: Marc Henri & Gaston Laverdet)

Webb Architects Ltd & Confederate Architects Ltd, London: Bruce Mackie 96, 139; William Tozer 126, 134

Richard Weston, Cardiff: 99TR, 108T

Acknowledgements

This book really represents the collective wisdom of designers and tutors within the industry whose generous contributions have made the whole project possible. I also have to thank the many KLC students and alumni who have generously allowed me to reproduce their work here to illustrate the text. I owe them all a huge debt of gratitude.

I would like to extend special thanks to Lizzie Stirrat on the KLC team who managed to persuade all and sundry to allow me to interview them for the book and carried out a great deal of valuable research which kept the project moving forward. Also at KLC, Rachel Neillie successfully overcame my lack of technical know-how and played a key role in rounding up all the illustrations and organizing the necessary photography. Diana McKnight, Jill Blake and Judy Jarman have been immensely supportive throughout the project, as has Simon Cavelle whose thought-provoking suggestions and contributions did so much to give the book a fresh slant.

I would particularly like to thank those designers and professional association members who took the time to express their views on specific areas or to provide quotes for the book: Bill Bennette, Helen Green, Kelly Hoppen, Kit Kemp of Firmdale Hotels, Noriko Sawayama, Philippa Thorp, Constanze von Unruh, Joanna Wood, Shirlee R Singer (ASID FIDEC), Maria Adelaida Rodriga (Member of CODDI – Colegio de Decoradores y Disenadores de Interiores de Puerto Rico), Manuel Francisco Jorge (IIDA Member Portugal), Lewis Goetz (President of IIDA), Monica Blinco, Shashi Caan (International Board of IIDA) and Eric Cohler.

After a lengthy telephone chat with Sue Crewe, editor of *House & Garden* magazine, I came away buzzing with new thoughts and ideas, while the input of Graham Merton of Eaton Gate Builders and the architects Peter Jones and Ron Lambell of Jones Lambell Architects helped me to provide a balanced view of the industry within the context of the book. Francis Binnington kindly contributed from the viewpoint of a decorative artist commissioned by an interior designer, and lighting consultant Rebecca Weir provided the lighting plans that appear in the book.

On the academic front, I am particularly indebted to Camilla Bunt of the Surrey Institute of Art & Design; Richard Sober, programme leader for Interior Architecture and Design and Interior Design at the School of Arts and Media at the University of Teeside; Peter Wheelwright, Chair of the Interior Design Programme at Parsons School of Design in New York; Anthony Feldman, Interior Design course director at the American International University in London; and Tatiana Rogova of Details Design School in Moscow. My thanks to all of these individuals for their thoughtful and constructive contributions.

I am very grateful to Martin Waller of Andrew Martin for giving me permission to use the excellent designer quotes from his latest *Interior Design Review* and, of course, to my patient and good-humoured editors Philip Cooper and Nell Webb who steered me through the project.

On the illustration front, I would like to thank the following KLC staff and students for allowing me to use their work in this book: Shanti Aldana, Isabelle Alfano, Jane Beaumont, Paul Biggs, Natasha Boutros, Isabel Campos, Samantha Crabb, Lisa Clowes, Camilla Corrigan, Laura Dansie, Stephanie Davis, Jo Davidson, Monica Day, Sally Dernie, Jana Durisova, Cynthia Garcia, Diane Horne, Kate Hildred, Julie Anne Jefferies, Julie Jeremy, Emily Keith, Steve Lait (in2style ltd), Zuzanna Lukacova, Anna Lindenberg, Isabel Maze, Kevin McEwen, Davina Merola, Svetlana Petrova, Olivia Pott, Hannah Rogers, Helen Smith, Antonia Stocker, Michelle Swaine, Debby Thurston, UDP Group, Jo Valensizi, Katharina Wachholtz, Marianne Walter Meaby and Tina Weaver.

No acknowledgement list would be complete without the inclusion of my very special husband, John, and all my family who patiently tolerated my fluctuating moods and humoured me until the job was done! This book is dedicated to them.